CAN YOU HELP POLICE
SOLVE THESE TRUE CRIMES?

WAS BUDDY JACOBSON INNOCENT? On the basis of a pair of bloodstained jeans later discovered to belong to someone else, top horse trainer Buddy Jacobson was convicted of killing the man who stole his girlfriend, a beautiful model. He died in prison protesting his innocence. His sister wants to clear his name. Reward: $5,000.

MURDER ON MUSIC ROW. Was it business or chance that ended the life of Kevin Hughes, country music chart director of *Cash Box* magazine? Dolly Parton's cousin found the body, and Nashville country superstars sang at the memorial service. The killer is still at large. Reward: $1,000.

ABDUCTION IN LAS VEGAS. It was his father's twenty-sixth birthday party, and by the middle of the night three-year-old Randi Layton Evers was missing—either taken or purchased by someone at the party. Was he sold for drugs or to settle a drug debt? Reward: $26,000.

FIND TIFFANY, INC. After Tiffany Sessions went out to jog and never returned, her father, Patrick, a Gainesville, Florida, businessman, enlisted the help of TV and sports celebrities and the governor himself to find her. Was she the victim of a serial killer? Or is she still alive? Reward: $250,000.

If you have any clues, you may be able to help

D1043521

For orders other than by individual consumers, Pocket Books grants a discount on the purchase of **10 or more** copies of single titles for special markets or premium use. For further details, please write to the Vice-President of Special Markets, Pocket Books, 1230 Avenue of the Americas, New York, NY 10020.

For information on how individual consumers can place orders, please write to Mail Order Department, Paramount Publishing, 200 Old Tappan Road, Old Tappan, NJ 07675.

REWARD!

PAULETTE COOPER and PAUL NOBLE

POCKET BOOKS

New York   London   Toronto   Sydney   Tokyo   Singapore

The sale of this book without its cover is unauthorized. If you purchased
this book without a cover, you should be aware that it was reported to
the publisher as "unsold and destroyed." Neither the author nor the publisher has received payment for the sale of this "stripped book."

An *Original* Publication of POCKET BOOKS

POCKET BOOKS, a division of Simon & Schuster Inc.
1230 Avenue of the Americas, New York, NY 10020

Copyright © 1994 by Paulette Cooper and Paul R. Noble

All rights reserved, including the right to reproduce
this book or portions thereof in any form whatsoever.
For information address Pocket Books, 1230 Avenue
of the Americas, New York, NY 10020

ISBN: 0-671-87020-3

First Pocket Books printing April 1994

10 9 8 7 6 5 4 3 2 1

POCKET and colophon are registered trademarks of
Simon & Schuster Inc.

Cover design by Tom McKeveny

Printed in the U.S.A.

To Bob and Sylvia Noble
and Suzy Eliya

Contents

CONTENTS

CONTENTS

Warning

Many of the people described in this book are dangerous.

Some are armed.

Do not approach or confront them.

Never try to apprehend a suspect yourself.

For your own safety and for the safety of others, don't take the law into your own hands.

If you have information about an unsolved case, call the number supplied here, write to the address given, or contact your local law enforcement officials. When possible, direct all of your inquiries to the organization or individual specified.

The publisher and authors do not warrant the terms or amounts of rewards offered by those listed here, and they assume no liability or responsibility for availability, payment, or nonpayment of rewards.

The publisher and authors do not offer protection to those whose furnishing of information puts them in jeopardy of the law, harassment, injury, or death.

Since the publication of this book, some individuals may already have been apprehended, certain cases may have been resolved or dismissed, and the rewards may have changed.

Introduction

Crime doesn't pay; helping to solve a crime can. The cases described in this book are true. All remain unsolved as of this writing, and all offer rewards. If you have information that can help resolve any of these crimes, please call the number listed in the "Reward" section at the end of each chapter. Not only might you earn some money—most rewards are in the $1,000–$25,000 range—you may also join in the fight against crime. The total amount of the rewards listed here is about three million dollars.

The crimes you will read about were allegedly committed by pedophiles, perverts, necrophiliacs, abductors, serial killers, serial rapists, serial kidnappers, terrorists, members of organized crime, highway harassers, jewel thieves, bank robbers, arsonists, hit-and-run drivers, and other dastardly criminals. Some of the victims disappeared in the twilight world of escort services, prostitution hangouts, outlaw motorcycle gangs, and sadomasochistic leather bars, and others became victims doing ordinary things such as jogging, driving, or delivering newspapers.

The victims range from a prostitute in Toronto to a child model in Texas to a Guardian Angel in New York

City, and the crimes took place all across North America, from Florida to British Columbia. We chose a wide variety of cases because we wanted to write an interesting crime book. We spoke to over three hundred people so that we could present each crime and investigation from a different angle. After all, if you just want the bare facts of a case, you can go to the post office and read the reward posters.

In presenting these individuals' stories, we included a generous sprinkling of quotes and let those involved speak for themselves. By doing this we hope you will get a feeling for the frustration of an investigator working on a long-term unsolved case, the anguish of a man searching for the murderer of his wife or the molester of his daughter, and a mother's torment as she agonizes over who killed her son—and why.

A lot of what these people say is not only moving but disturbing as well. We hope, however, that by presenting their experiences in this personalized manner, we can encourage you to come forward, not only if you have any information on *these* cases but if you have information on *any* crimes.

Rewards often aren't enough of an incentive to make someone divulge what he or she knows about a case. We hope that reading these incredible stories will sensitize you to the immense and intense anguish experienced by people who have lost loved ones to violence. Possibly you will then think twice in the future, not about whether to get involved in a crime investigation but whether to continue to remain silent if you know something that might lead to a solution.

There isn't enough space to thank all the reporters,

editors, investigators, detectives, police, public affairs officers, organizations (especially Crime Stoppers, Silent Witness, and other similar programs), missing children's support groups, private agents, public prosecutors, television programs (such as "Unsolved Mysteries," "A Current Affair," "Prime Suspect," and "America's Most Wanted"), magazines (*Crimebeat, Fugitive*), and newspapers throughout the country who tipped us off to cases or gave us background information about those we chose. We're also extremely grateful to our agent, Ted Chichak, and to Bill Grose and Molly Allen at Pocket Books.

Mostly, though, we thank each other for patience and assistance. We were initially wary about undertaking a project together, since we knew that collaborators often ended up refusing to talk to each other. Before we started this book, ours had been an extremely happy marriage. Now that we've finished this book, we are pleased to report that the description of our relationship remains the same.

Paulette Cooper and Paul Noble
July 1993

REWARD!

REWARD
$500,000 worth of land

The Model Shafaa

A strange thought went through Nancy Salem's mind when she first saw Deafallah Al Salem Falah. "I first spotted him in my church in El Paso, Texas, in the spring of 1980 when—lo and behold—here comes this man marching in with a big Bible in his hand. And I don't know why, but I immediately wondered, 'Is this the man God sent for me to marry?'"

The answer to that would turn out to be yes—a mistake that would ultimately lead Nancy to have to offer a reward worth approximately $500,000 for the safe return of their daughter, whom Deafallah had allegedly kidnapped. This, incidentally, is a real Texas-style reward. Nancy is offering property in Texas from which she says half a million dollars in minerals can be mined.

REWARD!

Nancy had a whirlwind romance with this mysterious Middle Easterner. "Like maybe two weeks. And then he flat out asked me to marry him.

"At first I was shocked. He was in his twenties, and I was in my early forties. But he said his prophet Mohammad's first wife was twenty years older than he was." Nancy's suitor also wasn't fazed when she told him she wasn't in love with him. "He said, 'In our culture we don't fall in love and get married. We get married and then fall in love.'"

Nancy's son by an earlier marriage would soon be leaving home to go to college, so, fearful of being lonely, Nancy Salem married Deafallah on May 13, 1980. "It was pitiful," she recalls. "Deafallah's clothes were too small on him, and he didn't even have a nice suit to get married. But I did plenty for him after we got married."

For example, when they first got married, "Deafallah worked for a trucking outfit, and there were difficulties. So I sent him to junior college, where he took computer courses. I really wanted him to feel good about himself."

But Nancy's new husband repaid her with abuse and accusations. What kept her from leaving the marriage was the birth on July 31, 1982, of her daughter Shafaa. Nancy hoped fatherhood would help her husband be more of a family man as well as the head of the family. Instead, he found himself a new family. "While he was at college he was meeting all these Arabs who were going there. One, a radical fanatic I'll call Ali, began to take over Deafallah's life."

Under the influence of Ali, "Deafallah quit going to

2

Nancy and Deafallah Salem
Photo courtesy of Nancy Salem

Shafaa Salem at age six
Photo courtesy of Nancy Salem

church with me" and tried to impose his beliefs on his daughter. For example, "When Shafaa was just six months of age, I put a little short dress on her. Deafallah looked at it and said her legs shouldn't be seen. For God's sake, she was a little baby."

Nancy bought a beautiful home for the three of them, sent Deafallah to real estate school, and bought a Middle Eastern restaurant in El Paso for him to run. Meanwhile, Shafaa was becoming a successful child model who won several beauty pageants. One day, when Deafallah was supposed to be taking their six-year-old child to school, he disappeared with her instead.

Nancy was frantic. "I called the U.S. Embassy, which found his parents living in a goatskin tent on the border of Syria and Jordan. I've also since learned that Shafaa has visited the Middle East with him. I'm afraid he may try to sell my daughter to a family over there that's got a lot of money, because she's strikingly beautiful."

So far, though, from other reports, her daughter appears to be safe and living in the United States. "One of Deafallah's Lebanese friends told me he saw Shafaa when she was briefly hiding out in a house with Deafallah. He said my daughter was wearing the long djellaba, right down to gloves covering her hands. He also made her cover that beautiful face. She's not even eleven yet," Nancy said.

Deafallah has been seen in the States in Houston, Dallas, and, as recently as September 1992, in Alexandria, Virginia. He's also been spotted in El Paso, Texas—with Shafaa—at the home of one of his friends. "Someone called me," Nancy said, "but the two had already left by the time the police and FBI got there at eleven-thirty at night."

Angrily, Nancy says, "They're very bold about what they do. One of Deafallah's friends called Shafaa's modeling teacher's brother, saying, 'Are you still looking for Deafallah? He's closer than you think.'"

Nancy has relieved her frustration by doing volunteer work for Mark Miller of the American Association for Lost Children, a nonprofit charity in Houston. So far, this Christian group has located sixty-five children—but unfortunately not Nancy's daughter.

"I've got Shafaa's clothes and her things in her room just like it was before, to help bring her memory back when she comes here," Nancy says. "And every birthday and holiday I buy a card and save it so I can show it to her when we get together.

"I've cried so hard over this I can hardly cry anymore. But I've got to go on and keep on top of this because these people have set out to destroy me. I won't let them, because I want to be around so I can get my daughter back," she vows.

Nancy says, "Shafaa looks older than her age. She's slender, has a heart-shaped scar almost in the middle of the bridge of her nose, brown hair, and brown eyes."

Deafallah, who is wanted by the FBI, goes under his real name as well as several aliases. He was born in 1957, is five feet five inches tall, weighs 155 pounds, has broad shoulders and a medium frame. He has a gap between his front teeth, black hair, and big brown eyes.

REWARD!

REWARD: Land valued at approximately $500,000 based on probable minerals that can be mined on it, according to Nancy Salem

FROM: Nancy Salem

FOR: The safe return of Shafaa Salem

CONTACT: Nancy Salem
 3100 McCann #202
 Longview, TX 75601

The above information is subject to the warning at the beginning of this book.

REWARD
$5,000

Westchester Gigolo

Before Cheryl Allen, a charming, pretty preschool teacher, learned the truth, she thought her twenty-three-year-old fiancé, Robert Freilich of Yonkers, New York, was every girl's dream. Handsome, with lots of money, and, Cheryl says, "wonderful in bed," Robert seemed an incredible catch.

It was after Robert turned up missing in October 1992 that his double life came out in the open. For Robert Freilich, a.k.a. Chris Lavae or Rob Lavae, turned out to be an exotic dancer and a hustler who "chaperoned" customers—male as well as female—for escort services. He was also a performer in porno-graphic films.

Cheryl Allen admits, "I knew him for two years and was engaged to him. I had no idea! I only learned about it all after he disappeared. His sister, who is a doctor, came to me and said, 'There's probably going to be things you'll learn that will make you uncomfortable.' I figured, okay, he probably had other girlfriends. Big deal! Just *find* him.

"I never, *ever* would have guessed him to be that way at all—an exotic dancer! A male escort! And for gay men! I was always worried about competition from other *girls,* but never did I think there were other *guys!*"

Still, she'd had some suspicions of a secret life earlier. "I didn't understand where he got all his money. He never would return his beeper calls in the evening. Obviously he was busy! If I was going to marry somebody, I wanted to know what he *did.* When he'd leave me at eleven and stay out until all hours, I kept asking him, 'What's going on?' He told me he was 'repossessing cars' and it had to be done at night. But everything begins to make sense now," Cheryl continues pensively.

"Robert's been doing this a long time," says his mother, Mrs. Judith Freilich. "He was getting good money being a chaperon to these people." When asked if she approved of that way of earning a living, she replies, "I don't know, I'm not that kind of person."

She's no longer entirely sure what kind of person her son Robert was by the time he disappeared on October 27, 1992. He and a friend met to go into nearby New York City. "He ended up in the Whiskey Bar in the theater district on Forty-sixth Street between Eighth Avenue and Broadway," Mrs. Freilich says. "He was supposed to meet a woman there named Bernadette. But he never met her." After nine, he was

REWARD!

Robert Freilich
Photo courtesy of Judith Freilich

seen there with a male about his height, a look-alike.
(Cheryl described Robert as muscular, 145 pounds,
clean-shaven, five feet six, with short brown hair and
brown eyes.) Robert left with this fellow about midnight. It was crowded, no one could identify the man
later.

"That was Tuesday night," his mother continues.
"Wednesday he didn't come home, although he said
he would, but one night away wasn't unusual. We don't
know what happened to him after he left the bar. His
car was found and impounded at nine in the morning."

REWARD!

When the Freilichs realized their son had left his beloved 1987 maroon Corvette, a substantial amount of money, his beautiful boat, his impressive jewelry collection, and his apartment's elegant furnishings—all his most prized possessions—they knew something was seriously wrong.

The Westchester police and renowned private investigator Irwin Blye are trying to track Robert down through bar owners and customers, pornography dealers and producers, male film theaters and burlesque houses, underground newspapers, hospitals, morgues, and escort services, where it was rumored that Robert earned $250 an hour. "Robert supposedly danced at a place called the Gaiety, which has male strippers," says investigator Blye.

Blye adds, "Robert wouldn't have left his car, his money, his clothes, and his personal items. And he loved his parents. It was a caring home.

"But in this double life he led, you never knew what kind of deals he was into," he continues. "He's a hustler, very charming, extremely good-looking, young and ballsy. He believes he can handle himself in the streets. He thinks of himself as a Romeo. I wonder if he ever saw *American Gigolo*. That's him, except, with his mindset, it's *both* ways."

Blye speculates, "Robert might have met up with a bad trick. Male or female, I don't know. He might have swindled someone who took vengeance on him. We have no body, so we don't know if he's alive or dead."

Cheryl believes that "maybe all the lying got to him and he went off to live the life he wanted to lead without anybody asking him questions.

REWARD!

"Or," she adds sorrowfully, "he's dead. Or in a situation he can't get out of." She admits she is still deeply in love with him. She thinks someone will spot him if he's alive because of one unique feature: his right eye doesn't move.

His mother wants him to return, too. "I don't know where the heck he disappeared to," she says. "You don't just drop your parents. I would give anything to get him back—regardless of what he had been doing."

REWARD: $5,000
FROM: The parents of Robert Freilich
FOR: Information leading to the return of Robert Freilich
CONTACT: Irwin Blye, Private Investigator
125-10 Queens Boulevard
Kew Gardens, NY 11415
Telephone: (718) 793-2005

The above information is subject to the warning at the beginning of this book.

REWARD
Unspecified
amount

3

The Southampton Fugitive

Don't expect to get close to William Peter Fischer and have him confess to you that he shot his handicapped son eighteen times at his lavish estate in Southampton, New York. For one thing, Fischer doesn't get close to *anyone*. "Some murderers are the kind to get drunk or upset and put their head on some girl's lap and start spilling the beans about the crimes they've committed," says New York State investigator John McGroary. "But Fischer's the kind of person who's never going to do that."

In fact, Fischer didn't even tell people he *had* a son and probably the last thing he would have told anyone is that there was something physically wrong with the boy.

Nineteen-year-old Bill—William Fischer, Jr.—suffered from cystic fibrosis, a genetic disease that clogs the lungs and usually shortens the victim's life, causing problems like pneumonia, chronic bronchitis, and malnutrition. The disease can sometimes be controlled with a special diet and proper medication, but that can be costly.

The cost of this medical treatment is suspected to be one reason why William Fischer probably killed his son.

Billy Fischer knew that his father, who lived in a $500,000 nine-room home in posh Southampton, had the means to help him. But Billy couldn't even get in touch with him to ask for money. "Fischer used a go-between whom his son would have to contact first because Fischer wouldn't let his son call him directly," McGroary says.

"He didn't want to have anything to do with his own son," McGroary continues, but somehow Billy inveigled an invitation to his father's Southampton home so the two of them could discuss his medical expenses. Since Billy didn't drive, the boy asked a friend, twenty-one-year-old bank clerk Nancy Hyer, to come along with him.

The visit appeared to start off well. A neighbor saw the three of them that afternoon, December 11, 1986, coming up the driveway. They were all cheerfully singing "Jingle Bells." However, Fischer had an unpredictable personality—although McGroary doesn't believe Fischer planned to murder his son. "William Fischer had a drug problem with cocaine. But something had to have happened that made him very angry or frustrated. Shooting someone eighteen times is done out of anger. It isn't necessary to shoot so many times to

REWARD!

William Peter Fischer
Photo courtesy of New York State Police

kill someone. Also, it probably wasn't premeditated
or he wouldn't have done it in his own home." Nancy
was also murdered, stabbed twice, her naked body
wrapped in a blanket.

When Nancy failed to return home the following
evening, her mother called the police. Investigators
found the two bodies in the trunk of Nancy Hyer's
car, parked behind the Elks Club in Southampton, near
Fischer's home. Billy's shirt had been pulled up
around his neck, his pants were ripped, and pebbles
were lodged in his buttocks, suggesting that this loving
father had dragged his son's body to Nancy's car.

Before the bodies were found, Fischer played the role of the worried parent. "When he was questioned, he was trying to be very helpful so we wouldn't suspect him of anything. He was a car dealer, so he was used to talking to people and getting them to relax," says McGroary.

"He also cried when talking to the police about his son. Fischer handed my partner a Mass card, one of those funeral cards, and wept. He said, 'Please capture the fiend who did this to my son.' Later we learned that Fischer could cry whenever he wanted to," says McGroary.

Fischer tried so hard to appear helpful that he even allowed the police to search his house without a warrant. "On January 17 he turned over his vacuum-cleaner bag." A big mistake. "In it was dried blood matching Miss Hyer's blood type, evidence that the girl had been in the house." Later the police found paint chips similar to those found on the blanket in which her naked body had been wrapped. And when the police sprayed the walls of Fischer's bedroom with a chemical that glows when it contacts blood, an unearthly glow emanated from the walls.

Fischer, realizing he was about to be arrested, took out a $160,000 loan against his house, supposedly to pay for his forthcoming legal defense. He persuaded his lawyer to make an oral agreement with the prosecutors that the lawyer would surrender Fischer voluntarily. The lawyer probably intended to do that, but when the time came for Fischer to be arrested, the lawyer said that he didn't know where his client was and that he was no longer representing him.

REWARD!

Fischer was last seen on February 10, 1987. Shortly thereafter, his blue Mercedes-Benz was found parked at Kennedy Airport. Says McGroary, "Even though he abuses alcohol and cocaine, he's proven in the past that he can keep a secret, so he'll never tell anyone the truth about himself. Even his ex-wives didn't know he had once done time in jail."

Fischer chain-smokes mentholated filter cigarettes, frequents waterfront areas, and gambles heavily, especially at roulette. He's five feet eleven inches tall and weighs 185 pounds. He has salt-and-pepper hair and blue eyes and a tracheotomy scar. The name "Mary" is tattooed on his right biceps.

McGroary has faith that Fischer will eventually be found. "You know how if you travel a lot, you go to a strange place and you bump into somebody that you went to school with or you met at a wedding?" asks McGroary. "Sooner or later somebody will bump into Fischer," he says hopefully.

R E W A R D : Unspecified amount
F R O M : New York State Police
F O R : Information leading to the arrest of William Peter Fischer
C O N T A C T : New York State Police
Telephone: 1-800-262-4321

The above information is subject to the warning at the beginning of this book.

REWARD
$25,000

4

The Murder of a Midwife

Although Martha Browning Bryant abhorred violence, the final year and a half of her life started and ended with death. It began when she and her husband of fifteen months rented their home in Portland, Oregon, only to learn that the local kids called the place Hell House. The neighbors' lame explanation was that the house number, 7734, when turned upside down, resembled the word "hell."

But Martha Bryant later found out that a gruesome murder-suicide had occurred in her bedroom two years earlier—and that the woman who had shot herself and her two daughters had gone to nursing school with Martha.

According to an account in the *Oregonian*, Martha was so spooked when she first learned this that she spent the night at Tuality Community Hospital, where

17

she had been midwifing a baby. Unfortunately she didn't choose to stay overnight on the night of October 8, 1992, even though she didn't finish work until 3:00 A.M. The forty-one-year-old first-time bride was anxious to get home to her new husband, so she leaped into her 1966 green Volkswagen Beetle, which she called Maggie after Maggie Simpson in "The Simpsons," and drove off down the main highway.

"Midwife by midlife" had been Martha's motto, and she had long since accomplished her goal, having delivered her 126th baby that night. She didn't seem to want children—for reporter Nena Baker, who investigated her background, found out that Martha had had her tubes tied years earlier. Nonetheless, Martha adored bringing other people's children into the world, and she jokingly said that one day she would open up her own low-cost clinic and call it The Elvis Presley Birthing Center.

On the night of October 8th she headed home, driving east on Cornell Road near Ray Circle. "A call came into our dispatch center saying they heard shots being fired in that area," says Detective Jeff Martin of the Hillsboro Police Department. The police located Martha's vehicle just a few miles from the hospital on the opposite side of the road. There they found "ten holes from the passenger's side and no one inside."

Reconstructing the crime, the police established that a car with two occupants had shot at Martha with a semiautomatic pistol or an assault rifle, forcing her car off the road. The gunmen then took the terrified midwife into their own car, drove about a third of a mile away, and attempted to rape her. Finally they shot her in the head and shoulder with a .22 gun and dumped her, half dead, in the middle of a deserted road.

Martha was found by a motorist and flown to the same hospital where she had studied midwifery. But those who had taught her to save others' lives were unable to save hers. Martha Browning Bryant died two hours later, near the maternity ward where she had trained.

There were a few clues to this murder. When the gunmen forced Martha off the road, the occupant of a nearby house was "awakened from sleep as a result of hearing the shots being fired," says Detective Martin. "And she [the neighbor] looks out and sees a white male adult in his twenties, about six feet tall, with a medium build and wavy brown hair, cut short, standing.

"And she hears a second voice and knows that at least two people are involved. She hears their car, and it had a throaty sound and a shiny appearance, as if the person took good care of it. It was well tuned with a powerful engine, what they call a muscle-type car. It's light colored, possibly white or silver, late sixties or early seventies, two doors, similar to a 1967 Chevelle or a 1968 Olds 442 or Pontiac Le Mans."

The police were also able to establish the type of Saturday night special that killed Martha. It was "of a type that hasn't been sold new in the United States since the sixties or seventies," says Detective Martin. "They don't even make these kinds of guns anymore, and there are only six manufacturers for this gun, and these are not common names."

REWARD!

Ballistics analysis indicates that the fatal gunshot came from a .22 revolver made by one of these six manufacturers: Herbert Schmidt, Rohm (Model RG-10, RG-15, RG-20, RG-15 .22 revolver or .22 Derringer), RG Industries (Model RGU-2, RG-10), Liberty Arms (Model 21), EIG (Model E1), and EMGE.

The police and the public are baffled as to why someone would commit such a crime in this manner. "If they wanted to kill the driver, why extract her off the major roadway where there's a residential neighborhood? Why wouldn't they wait until she reached a remote area?" Detective Martin asks.

"There was no apparent reason," he says. "We found her purse inside the vehicle, which would probably rule out a robbery attempt." Then the detective added philosophically, "Here you have a woman who brings a life into the world, and within an hour or two somebody takes hers away. It makes no sense."

Update

On April 29, 1993, a grand jury in Washington County, Oregon, handed down indictments against thirty-two-year-old Cesar Francesco Barone in the slaying of Martha Browning Bryant. Barone, who has also used the name of Adolph James Rode, had been picked up on charges of attempted rape and burglary in another case and has also been indicted in a second slaying, as well as being a "person of interest" in other killings. The state says that if he is convicted, it will seek the death penalty against Barone in the case of

REWARD!

Martha Bryant, whom he appears to have attacked randomly.

However, the reward on this case was still outstanding in 1993, and information is being sought about Barone's activities and the vehicles operated by him. And information is still being sought as to the identity of the second suspect in the murder of the midwife.

REWARD: $25,000
FROM: $15,000 Tuality Community Hospital, plus contributions from Friends and Crimestoppers, $10,000
FOR: Information leading to the arrest and conviction of the murderer or murderers of Martha Browning Bryant
CONTACT: Detective Jeff Martin or Sergeant Tom Robinson
Hillsboro Police Department
Telephone: (503) 681-6175

The above information is subject to the warning at the beginning of this book.

REWARD
$1,000

5

Soon to Be a TV Movie of the Week

Who says nothing ever happens on a fifteen-year-old case? The story of twenty-two-year-old Patricia Kisner was so interesting that "A Current Affair" resurrected it in 1992. After the show was aired, a witness came forward with some new information—but there's still not quite enough evidence to charge anyone.

Las Vegas Police Detective Tom Dillard tells what he knows of the bizarre story: "Patricia Kisner, a young married woman with a baby, was complaining of a stomach disorder in general terms," he says. She went to a gynecologist, Dr. William Harrison, who she later claimed had misdiagnosed her ailment, and she underwent a series of X-rays and barium studies. As it turned out, she was pregnant, but as a result of the X-rays she decided to abort the baby.

Patricia was furious at the doctor's misdiagnosis. She retaliated by going "to the Nevada Medical Board as well as filing a civil suit against the doctor," says Detective Dillard. Then Patricia started receiving mysterious phone calls at her home from a male who identified himself as an IRS agent. He told Patricia he wanted her to get a job working on the strip doing "tip checks" to see if people were declaring all their income. Since the IRS doesn't solicit people for jobs, and since no such job exists, it is highly likely someone was trying to find out when Patricia would be home alone.

"The suit was pending, and the medical board hearing was due within a few days when Patricia was found dead on August 23, 1978," continues Dillard. Patricia's husband had come home to find his wife, naked from the waist down. She had been shot twice in the head with a small-caliber weapon.

"The crime scene and the position of the body would lead one to immediately suspect a . . . home-intrusion sexual-assault crime," Dillard says. Although semen was found on the scene, "there was no proof of intercourse." In fact, there was no proof of anything. "The investigation pretty much was at a stalemate from that point on," the detective admits.

Then, about a year later, the wife of the doctor Patricia had been suing "came forward with startling information," continues Dillard. Victoria Harrison claimed that her husband, disguised in a long wig and wearing hippie clothes, had murdered Patricia Kisner, purposely leaving semen behind, probably to mislead prosecutors into believing it was a sex crime. According to Victoria Harrison, her husband had obtained the semen from "samples from vasectomies that he performed in his office," says Dillard. "Victoria told the detectives that he [the doctor] kept the semen" in the refrigerator. Dillard tried to establish the truth of her claim by testing the semen for DNA. "But it's untypable, which didn't surprise me. Everybody thinks DNA is a panacea. It's not. I was looking to determine if it [the semen] could have been from multiple donors, but there's no way to tell."

Despite Victoria's charges, the doctor couldn't be prosecuted on the basis of his wife's statement without a corroborating witness. However, after fifteen years, people are now starting to talk. To the police. To "A Current Affair." To producers who plan to make a TV movie out of this story. Even to the accused doctor. "A Current Affair" confronted Dr. Harrison and asked him whether his wife had made a statement implicating him. "I think she did, but there was nothing to it," he replied.

"There's no 'think,'" says Dillard angrily. "There's no question that she [Victoria] made the statement. His attorney was provided with a copy of it." Dr. Harrison has not been charged and maintains his innocence. "I know I had nothing to do with it," he said when questioned by "A Current Affair."

REWARD: $1,000
FROM: Secret Witness
FOR: Arrest and indictment of the murderer or murderers of Patricia Kisner
CONTACT: Secret Witness
Telephone: (702) 385-5555

The above information is subject to the warning at the beginning of this book.

REWARD
Up to $13,000

_____ **6**

Girls, Ghouls,
and Graves

Tim Bindner, a former cemetery worker and cremato-
rium operator, visits graveyards four or five evenings
a week. In 1986 this Berkeley graduate lost his job at
the Social Security Administration because he was, by
his own admission, "sending unsolicited gifts of money
and birthday cards to some girls in Colorado whose
names I got out of Social Security files."

Questions about this forty-four-year-old waste-water
treatment plant operator began to arise in 1988. Sergeant Mark Fwazi of the San Pablo police answered
a call from two girls who complained about harassment. Fwazi investigated and was chilled when he
found that the interior of Bindner's van was decorated
with dozens of color and black-and-white photographs
of young girls, seven to thirteen years old—photos that
had come from missing-children bulletins.

Currently, the cases of five missing California girls—all unsolved abductions—seem to have some connection to Bindner. He says his only reason for keeping the macabre photo collection in his van and his home is to help recover kidnapped children. That's why he says he has helped search for them, sent them letters after they were found dead, and visited their graves. .

Many people are worried about Bindner—very worried. One such person is the mother of Amanda Nicole "Nikki" Campbell, a four-year-old girl who was last seen on Friday, December 27, 1991. It was raining when the dimpled, blond, blue-eyed daughter of Walter and Mary Ann Campbell disappeared while on her way to a friend's house in Fairfield, California. Her bicycle was later found along a small grassy area on nearby Norwalk Place.

Mary Ann Campbell told the Fairfield *Republic* that her daughter wasn't afraid to talk to strangers and could hold a mature conversation with an adult, something that appears to be true of many abducted children. Boston private investigator Gil Lewis feels that "this maturity lulls parents into a false note of complacency that the child can handle itself like an adult. The parents forget that they're babies and as portable as turkeys."

When Detective Harold Sagan and the Fairfield police searched the Oakland home of Tim Bindner to look for evidence, they took away four cartons of materials from this grave-lover, but they left him unarrested. Ten days after Nikki's disappearance, the police used dogs to try to track her scent. The dogs sniffed around uninterested until Tim Bindner walked

REWARD!

Amanda "Nikki" Campbell
Photo courtesy of Fairfield, California, Department of Public Safety

out of a nearby ditch a block away from Nikki's house.
The dogs leaped up on Bindner and seemed to pick up
Nikki's scent on his car, a green Toyota Corolla.

Dogs may have tracked down Bindner on another
occasion as well. Detective Harold Sagan wonders
whether Bindner took Nikki to the grave of a girl, An-
gela Bugay, who had been abducted in Antioch, California, nine years earlier, because a police bloodhound
also found Nikki's scent at Bugay's grave. Drinking
straws and french fry wrappers were found in Bind-

ner's cluttered van, leading police to think that Bindner might have taken Nikki to McDonald's before driving her to the cemetery.

There are other curious connections as well. For several months Bindner had been sending nonthreatening letters to a twelve-year-old girl who lived one block from Nikki—but forty miles from his own home in Oakland. Detective Sagan thinks Bindner may have been looking for the twelve-year-old in that Fairfield neighborhood when he came upon Nikki.

Another coincidence is that Bindner was one of the first to help in the search for a missing child named Amber Jean Swartz-Garcia in June of 1988 (see Chapter 54). Bindner also joined the search team for Nikki Campbell. As Nikki's mother asked on CBS's "Street Stories" in February 1993, "Would you want some stranger you don't even know looking for your child? No, you wouldn't. I don't want someone looking for my daughter whom I don't know."

"Tim Bindner is our number one prime suspect in the abduction of Nikki Campbell . . . based on evidence that we hold," Detective Sagan says bluntly. Sagan speculates that Bindner, while looking for the unnamed twelve-year-old girl he was sending letters to, could have abducted Nikki, taken her to his car, and then driven onto a main thoroughfare connecting with a major freeway only a mile away. "So within just a couple of minutes he was totally out of town, child in hand."

"There is so much more about this guy that has never been made public," says Sagan. He believes the reason underlying Nikki's abduction was sexual, "because we're dealing with a stranger abduction. There's a greater likelihood the abduction was for sexual abuse." He said of Nikki, "She was in the wrong place at the wrong time."

Tim Bindner has a reply to all this. He told interviewer Richard Roth on "Street Stories," "Harold Sagan has put together a theory. And he can put together another thousand theories about what happened to this child. His theory is just plain false. . . . It is true that somebody that hangs around graveyards, that goes in graveyards at night, somebody that visits the grave of a murdered child that he didn't ever know, is someone that would make the police suspicious, and I just have to live with that."

Nikki Campbell was three feet six and weighed 55 pounds. She was last seen wearing a pink jacket, a purple short-sleeve top, purple pants, and white tennis shoes. Her disappearance is the most recent of a series of stranger abductions that have struck northern California families over the last four years.

"These other parents are turning to me for salvation," says Harold Sagan. "They believe that Tim did it. . . . This stuff happens, folks. This is real life.

"We hope to resolve this soon," adds Sagan.

REWARD: Up to $13,000
FROM: Fairfield, California, Department of Public Safety
FOR: Information leading to the recovery of Nikki Campbell
CONTACT: Fairfield, California, Department of Public Safety
Telephone: (707) 428-7364

The above information is subject to the warning at the beginning of this book.

REWARD
Unspecified
amount

7

To Catch a
Jewel Thief

If there is such a thing as a nice jewel-theft gang, then this was it. According to Special Agent Mike Driscoll of the Florida Department of Law Enforcement, the four robbers "never hurt anybody. They did not want a confrontation; they just wanted to rob the jewelry store and make easy money with no problems. They sometimes said, 'Thank you, ma'am,' after they took jewelry from a female clerk."

This quartet specialized in stealing from jewelry shops in shopping malls because, says Driscoll, "It's easier to mix and blend into a crowd in a mall; the parking lot areas may be crowded, making escape easier, and they can study the jewelry store in advance from another shop in the mall without being seen."

The only one of the four with a criminal record was the gang leader, Robert Mire, who also used the name

REWARD!

James Strongin. Mire had been brought up in Palm Beach County, Florida, and while serving a five-year jail sentence, walked out of a work-release program in 1987. After he got out, Mire put together the rest of his gang, which included thirty-seven-year-old Mark Anthony Wade and two others.

Starting in 1988 the four of them began hitting mall jewelers every three to six months. They lived lavishly when they had a good score, staying in top hotels, buying Corvettes, and wearing expensive jewelry, some of which came from their robberies. When their money got low, they'd do some research and then hit another jewelry store.

This gang always cased places before they hit them. Driscoll says, "They were looking for escape routes, security guards, and whether or not they were armed, or if the police officers in the mall actually handled the security. Before they hit a place they also checked on the number of employees on duty, when they were there, how many surveillance cameras they had, and where they were located."

They usually worked together, but Mark Wade—the gang member for whom there is a reward—committed a few robberies alone. At least one he botched quite badly. At Mayor's Jewelry Store in Fort Lauderdale, his first visit to the place was in a disguise so obvious that he immediately aroused suspicion.

Detective Donald McCawley of the Fort Lauderdale Police Department has been investigating that robbery. (McCawley, incidentally, has encountered unusual perpetrators before. He sniffed out the "Stinky Bandit," a bank robber with such egregious body odor that bank employees rapidly turned over all their money to him to get out of the place!)

During this robbery, McCawley says, "Wade looked like he had put these things in his cheeks [to make his face look fatter]; he was wearing fake eyeglasses and a bad toupee. The clerks stared at him and thought he looked like a weird individual."

A couple of weeks after this initial attention-getting visit, "this eccentric-looking guy comes back looking even stranger, with a longer wig. A clerk thought she recognized him from his earlier visit, but Mayor's has a high-class kind of clientele, and they don't want to ring alarms and have the police scare away a legitimate customer. So they hemmed and hawed. Suddenly Wade presented a gun under his jacket" and made off with a million and a half dollars' worth of goods.

But Wade made two mistakes. True, there was no surveillance camera in the store, but there was one in the mall. While Wade had been casing the place in his obvious disguise, his picture was taken. A bizarre-looking guy in an obvious disguise was easy to zero in on later.

Worse still, when Wade entered the store, "He was drinking out of a cup that he got in the mall. And when he ran out with the diamonds, he left his cup on the counter—with his fingerprints right on it."

Although this was later used as proof that Wade was the perpetrator, it didn't help in catching him then, for Wade had no criminal record to which those prints could be matched. ("It's not like we find prints and match them to everyone in the world," explains Driscoll.) Meanwhile, Wade continued to carry out more

REWARD!

Mark Anthony Wade
Photo courtesy of Florida Department
of Law Enforcement

successful heists with his gang. This gang has "hit all over the state of Florida," Driscoll says, and Wade has been tracked out to California as well.

The first member of the gang was caught when he pawned some stolen Rolex watches in Miami. Through him they caught a second gang member. "But he didn't know where Wade and Mire were because they lived in hotels, used fake IDs, and didn't work," says Driscoll. "It was like trying to find a ghost," he says.

Robert Mire, a.k.a. James Strongin, was eventually tracked down at a gun show on December 7, 1991. "He was spotted and, with guns drawn, the police shouted, 'Mire, freeze. You're under arrest.' Mire ran about fifty feet, stopped, pulled a gun out of his waistband, and put the gun to his temple."

REWARD!

After Mire's suicide, only Wade was left. Mark Wade is one of Florida's eight most wanted criminals. He is five feet eight inches tall, weighs about 150 pounds, and has brown hair and brown eyes. "Sometimes he has a mustache and sometimes he doesn't," says Driscoll. "Although he comes from Niagara Falls, he occasionally speaks with a British accent. He often uses the alias Mark Swain.

"He takes antidepressant drugs and has told people that he has AIDS and/or that he's HIV-positive.

"In the past, and probably now, he's involved in musical groups as a lead guitarist. He's probably in Florida or California right now," Driscoll surmises. Even though he and his gang didn't shoot anybody, Wade is considered armed and dangerous and is known to wear a bulletproof vest.

Says Driscoll, "I often get Wade sightings [that turn out to be people who look like him]. If he's working legitimately, he may be selling advertising balloons or working as an engineer in a recording studio. But he may still be robbing jewelry stores."

If so, he may be working alone now.

REWARD: Unspecified amount
FROM: Florida Department of Law Enforcement
FOR: The apprehension of Mark Anthony Wade
CONTACT: Mike Driscoll, special agent for the Florida Department of Law Enforcement
Telephone: 1-800-226-1514 or
(407) 468-5692

The above information is subject to the warning at the beginning of this book.

REWARD
$80,000

8

A Flight Attendant's Final Trip

Nancy Ludwig, age forty-one, had been a flight attendant for fifteen years, first for Republic Airlines and then with Northwest after it merged with Republic. On the weekend of her death, Nancy was an add-on flight attendant, a substitute for others on various routes.

On Sunday, February 17, 1991, she flew from Las Vegas to Detroit and stayed overnight at the 268-room Hilton Airport Inn in Romulus, Michigan, just north of the Detroit Metropolitan Airport. On Monday she was to continue to Fort Lauderdale, Memphis, and Indianapolis before returning home.

The Hilton Airport Inn is a popular place for airline personnel. An average of 50 to 190 Northwest flight attendants and crew stay there every night, providing the hotel with approximately 95 percent of its business.

Nancy checked in at nine o'clock Sunday evening and failed to respond to wake-up calls the following morning. However, since she was an add-on, no other crew members were assigned to check on her or travel with her to the airport, so no one looked in on her. It was only when a housekeeper opened the door to her third-floor room at 1:00 P.M. that Nancy's naked body, bound and gagged, was found lying on the floor.

Her body had multiple stab wounds, and her throat had been cut. The room was spattered with blood. Evidence showed that she had been raped twice. According to Sergeant Dan Snyder of the Romulus Police Department, she may have been raped both before and after she was killed.

Police found no sign of forced entry into the hotel room. Unfortunately that isn't unusual, for all too many women traveling alone have become victims— usually of robbery or rape rather than murder—after responding to innocent-sounding requests from men on the other side of the door who pose as hotel security or maintenance personnel.

"The front desk sent me to look at a leak in the sink," is enough to make many women naively open their door to a total stranger. Some attackers use house phones to pave the way, psychologically disarming their intended victims by posing as someone from the front desk: "We're sending somebody up to check on the TV"—and the occupant immediately opens the door to the next person who knocks.

In this case the police ruled out a social visit. They found no signs of food or drink in the room. No weapon and no fingerprints were found in the room

Nancy Ludwig
Photo courtesy of
Arthur A. Ludwig

**Police sketch of man
who rode in airport
van to hotel with
Nancy Ludwig**
Sketch courtesy of
Romulus, Michigan,
Police Department

either. Says Sergeant Snyder, "An unusual thing about this case is that everything she owned and had with her was taken. All of her jewelry, luggage, airline identification materials, her earrings, two expensive diamond rings, the clothing she was wearing," including her undergarments.

"They still exist somewhere as trophies," ventures Nancy's fifty-nine-year-old husband, Art Ludwig, who had been married to her for thirteen years at the time of the murder and is a retired program director for the NBC television affiliate in Minneapolis.

There were only two clues to the murder. A female flight attendant who accompanied Nancy Ludwig on a shuttle van ride from Northwest Airlines to the hotel in Romulus said there was one other passenger on that bus trip. The man was about forty-five years old, and of average height. The flight attendant said the man stared at Nancy for the duration of the ride.

"There were three double seats in the van behind the driver," explains Sergeant Snyder. "Normally, if there are three people, they each take a seat of their own. In this case, the man took a seat right next to Nancy and stared at her all the way to the hotel."

In addition, another witness saw a man putting Northwest-type luggage into the trunk of a late-model Monte Carlo at about 10:15 P.M. Sunday evening— right after Nancy was probably murdered. The police are still studying people who were released from nearby mental hospitals because of budget cuts. They also continue to scrutinize workers at nearby hotels and at other service industries.

"I never knew what was going on in the world until

REWARD!

**Police sketch of man seen putting Northwest-type
luggage into trunk of Monte Carlo at 10:15 Sunday evening**
Sketch courtesy of Romulus, Michigan, Police Department

this happened to us," says Nancy's bereaved husband,
Art Ludwig. "When you get involved in a crime like
this, yours never seems to be solved, and everyone
else's does. There have been many strange murders in
Minneapolis, and the police managed to find all the
other killers," he says bitterly.

"I've been trying to get the public involved," continues this man who now devotes all of his time in Minne-
tonka, Minnesota, where he lives, trying to help find
his wife's killer. "We're actually no further now than
we were two years ago. Somebody's got to know something."

REWARD!

REWARD: $80,000
FROM: Nancy's husband, the television station where he worked, the Hilton Hotel chain, and Teamsters Union officials
FOR: Information leading to the arrest and conviction of the suspect wanted for the slaying of Nancy Ludwig
CONTACT: Detective Dan Snyder
Romulus, Michigan, Police
Telephone: (313) 942-6855

The above information is subject to the warning at the beginning of this book.

REWARD
$36,000

9

Passing on the Parkway

The peace of Christmas night 1992 was shattered for accountant John Mascaro and his family when his wife, Pamela, was shot to death as they drove home from a celebration on Long Island.

At about ten o'clock that Christmas night, John Mascaro was driving westbound on the Grand Central Parkway in Queens, New York. "I was just going along with the traffic and moving out of the way of any car going faster," he recalls. "I was in the left lane for twenty minutes to a half hour, doing about sixty-five miles an hour."

Between the Lakeville Road and the Little Neck Road exits he noticed a "fairly small vehicle tucked very tightly behind me on my rear bumper." The car was white, ivory, or bone-colored and boxy-looking with a squared-off front, like a foreign compact or midsize car, perhaps a Toyota Celica, Nissan, or Mitsubishi. John slowed down slightly by tapping a couple of times on his brakes.

The other driver appeared "very impatient and immediately drove off to my right side into the middle lane. He came up parallel to me. There was no exchange of words. We gesticulated at each other," he said politely, meaning he and the other driver did what many would do in such a situation—they gave each other the finger.

At this point Mascaro got his first close-up glance at his nemesis. "He definitely looked like an emotionally disturbed hyper person," he recalls. "I think he was fairly large, especially relative to the size of his car. My first thought was that his face gave the appearance of being distorted."

But then Mascaro was shocked to see that "the man was wearing something like a nylon stocking as a mask. At that point the masked man slowed down into my right-hand blind spot. Then I heard the first gunshot. I think he was aiming for my tires." The shot ricocheted under the rear passenger seat, where Mascaro's three-year-old daughter, Holly, sat.

Additional shots "blew out the front right passenger window and the rear windshield," he recalled. Terrified, he knew he had to escape, but "I couldn't swerve my car left because of the divider. I couldn't go right because of the gunman in the middle lane. Also, I saw there was another car in the right lane. I began to think this was the end."

He turned and saw that his daughter, clutching her Little Mermaid dolls, was unhurt, but when he looked

Pamela, Holly, and John Mascaro
Photo courtesy of John Mascaro and the Savino family

to his right, John was horrified to see his wife, Pam, slumped down. He reached over to touch her head and saw there was blood.

Mascaro barreled up a jammed exit ramp, traveling mainly on the grass to avoid hitting stopped cars. Somehow he managed to screech into a gas station and demand help.

"This kind black gentleman, a beautiful human being, was getting gasoline. Together we held my wife's hands and prayed. I was still sitting, stunned, in the driver's seat. I could hear Pam's muffled breathing and gurgling. As the paramedics took her away, I said, 'God, I'll be your servant for the rest of my life if you can perform a miracle and save my wife's life!'"

Pamela was put on life-support systems, but she

died at 10:25 the next night. Holly Mascaro, who had been in the back seat of the car, had been sprayed by glass when the shot came through the window, but she was uninjured.

Over the next few days many people reported similar harassment from what seemed to be the same car on the parkway, although no one else was shot. "He was high-beaming them," Mascaro said. "He was looking to push somebody to the edge."

"Sometimes people don't realize that they might hold a small bit of information," says New York City Police Sergeant John Russell, commanding officer of the 111th Precinct detective squad. "To them, it's so minute, it really doesn't mean anything. To the police, it might be the piece of the puzzle we're looking for. One or two license-plate numbers, not even the whole license number."

Unfortunately it will be too late to help Pam Mascaro. She and John had been a storybook couple. John's family had fled Cuba in the early days after Castro's rise to power, and he had met Pam in high school. They attended St. John's University together and had been married for nine years.

Losing his wife was hard enough for John Mascaro, but then he had to explain her absence to his daughter. One Saturday morning a few weeks after Christmas, they were watching cartoons on television together when once again Holly asked, "Where's Mommy?"

"I sat her on my lap and lowered the TV," Mascaro recounts. "I said, 'Dada has to tell you something, and I don't want you to be afraid and take it the wrong way. Mommy died. She's not coming back anymore.'"

He saw that Holly's eyes were beginning to fill with tears.

"'You won't be able to see her or touch her like you can do to Dada, but I want you to know that she always loves you. She's going to be with us forever. We'll pray for her, for she is with God, and God loves us all, and God is taking care of her. If you need anything, come to me.'

"Even though she's so small," he continues, "she feels very grown up knowing that I told her the truth. I never make her think that her mother's gone away from her life.

"There's a reason for good things to happen and a reason for bad things," he said philosophically. "We don't always know the answers on this earth. One day we will realize God's plan was well intentioned even though it seemed at the time to be very painful."

REWARD: $36,000
FROM: The Office of the Mayor of the City of New York, $10,000; Crimestoppers, $1,000; Pamela Mascaro's father, $25,000
FOR: Information leading to the arrest and conviction of the killer of Pamela Mascaro
CONTACT: Crimestoppers
　　　　　　　Telephone: (212) 577-TIPS

The above information is subject to the warning at the beginning of this book.

A special scholarship fund for Holly Mascaro has been set up by Price Waterhouse. Donations can be mailed to John O. Hatab, Price Waterhouse, 45th floor, 1177 Avenue of the Americas, New York, NY 10036.

REWARD
$5,000

10

Was Buddy Jacobson Innocent?

Howard "Buddy" Jacobson seemed to have everything anyone could ever want in life—until he ended up in jail. He had started out raking stables and had worked his way up to become one of the top horse trainers in the country. He was rich, and he had a dazzling woman on his arm, beautiful cover girl Melanie Cain, with whom he also ran a successful modeling agency.

All that was to change after a tenant named Jack Tupper and a few of his friends moved into the Manhattan apartment building at 121 East Eighty-fourth Street that Buddy lived in and owned. Melanie, who had lived there with Buddy sporadically for five years, immediately fell for Tupper.

As if that wasn't bad enough for Buddy, shortly thereafter he found himself accused of having murdered Tupper because of a supposed love triangle. During his trial, the most damaging evidence against him was a pair of blue jeans he was supposedly wearing on the day Tupper disappeared. The D.A.'s office said the jeans had blood on them—something that Buddy could never explain.

The state thought it could. It charged that at 10:30 A.M. on Sunday, August 6, 1978, Jack Tupper, former owner of the All Ireland bar, was murdered by Buddy Jacobson in Buddy's apartment building. They said Buddy then disposed of Tupper's body at a Bronx dump site. The case against Buddy was mostly circumstantial, based primarily on his bloody jeans and the assertion that he had been at the Co-op City Dumpster shortly after the body of Jack Tupper was found there.

Buddy knew there were many others who might have wanted to kill Jack Tupper, a shady character who was peripherally involved in a major drug case. But the public and the jury never saw that side of Tupper. He was presented only as a victim and a respectable restaurateur. In fact, Tupper was charged as a conspirator in a case against the infamous Don Brown gang, sometimes called the Irish Mafia, a group involved in the Lufthansa cargo heist at Kennedy Airport in December of 1978.

Buddy, on the other hand, found himself depicted as the bad guy, not just by Melanie, whom he loved, but by the D.A.'s office, which was out to get him, and by a public that had already convicted him of murder before a jury did so at his arduous three-month trial.

He was sentenced to a minimum of twenty-five years, but in a sensational move, he escaped and fled

REWARD!

Buddy Jacobson
Photo courtesy of the family of Howard "Buddy" Jacobson

to California. There he tried to track down the evidence he needed to prove Tupper was a drug dealer. Before he had the chance, however, the D.A.'s office coerced Buddy's own son into turning his father in. Once more Buddy was back in jail.

There he languished for ten long years. "The evidence against him was deadly," says his sister, Rita Costello, who has worked tirelessly throughout the years to try to clear her brother's name. "Everything pointed to his guilt—but then it started to unravel."

It unraveled when, once again, Rita was poring over Buddy's voluminous legal papers. On her own, she had been trying to find evidence of her brother's innocence. "Suddenly I noticed that the police ID number of Buddy's bloodstained blue jeans was not the same as the number on his other clothes," she says excitedly.

Checking further, she learned that the jeans said to be Buddy Jacobson's actually belonged to a painter who had been arrested with him and then released. "The jeans they used in court really belonged to this other man," she says, glancing around with blue eyes that look just like Buddy's. "The numbers were only one digit apart." When she investigated further, she learned that "the ones actually belonging to Buddy had tested negative for blood."

Eight years after the trial, Rita Costello was still going through legal papers, calling every person mentioned in the police records to see if any of them had any information that might help her brother.

Suddenly she came upon a name in the police files that she hadn't seen before: Cecilia Linzie. Rita called her and was shocked to hear Linzie say that she had told the police the day after the murder that she had seen three men at the dump site where Tupper's body was found. When the police showed her a photograph of Buddy Jacobson, she had indicated that none of the men she had seen looked like the photo they showed her. But she was never asked to testify.

That Tupper was killed because of his drug activities is a more believable scenario than that Buddy, a five-foot eight-inch tall, 135-pound man, killed Tupper, who weighed 215 pounds and was six feet two. Moreover, Tupper was a brown belt karate expert and a wrestling champion! Buddy supposedly shot Tupper eight times, then stabbed him six times, and finally hit him over the head with a heavy instrument, yet Jacobson didn't have a single mark on him afterward; the only sign of violence was the blood on those jeans.

There is more evidence of Buddy's innocence, but none of it will ever be heard by a jury. Buddy died on May 16, 1989, one day before the New York State Appellate Court was about to hear about the newly discovered evidence.

Buddy Jacobson finally did get out of jail after ten years—in a box. The last words on his lips were protestations of his innocence.

To encourage someone to come forward with the truth so she can clear her brother's name, Rita Costello is offering a $5,000 reward for information about the actual circumstances of Jack Tupper's death.

REWARD: $5,000
FROM: Rita Costello
FOR: Information conclusively identifying the killer of Jack Tupper or conclusively establishing Buddy Jacobson's innocence
CONTACT: Diarmuid White
Lipsitz, Green, Fahringer, Roll, Salisbury
& Cambria
110 E. 59th St.
New York, NY 10022-1304

The above information is subject to the warning at the beginning of this book.

REWARD
$26,000

11

Not a Happy Birthday Party

The first anyone knew about a tale that would have Las Vegas talking—and it takes a lot to get Las Vegans talking about anything other than gambling—was when Carri Geer of the Las Vegas *Review-Journal* wrote a story headlined "Three-Year-Old Disappears in Middle of the Night."

The reason everyone was talking was that this was not an ordinary abduction report. No one knew for sure *what* it was. For Randi Layton Evers may still be alive someplace, having been taken—or purchased— by someone who attended a birthday party on February 15, 1992, on East Rochelle Avenue in Las Vegas.

Just as this wasn't an ordinary abduction, it wasn't a typical birthday party. The fete was supposed to begin on Saturday at 7:30 P.M., but guests started arriving at 4:30. A few of them were so eager to wish

REWARD!

Michael Evers—a roofer who is the missing child's natural father—a happy twenty-sixth birthday that they even flew in from Los Angeles for the gathering. The party was supposedly over at 11:30, although several of those who attended stayed in the two-bedroom apartment, where five people were already living.

What happened during the night has never been clear. The birthday boy, Michael Evers, later told the police that by 11:00 P.M. he had consumed four beers. Exhausted, he climbed onto a double mattress on the floor of the apartment's front bedroom and fell into a

Randi Evers
Photo courtesy of Nevada Child Seekers

deep sleep. Michael said that when he last saw his three-foot-tall, 50-pound blond, blue-eyed son, Randi, the boy was curled up under a blanket in the living room in front of the apartment. He was wearing a black shirt and blue pants with diamonds on the knees.

Michael's twenty-two-year-old wife, Tina, who is Randi's stepmother, said she left the apartment with five of the guests around 11:30 that night to gamble. When she returned about three hours later, she said Randi was gone. After searching the area, she called the police at 4:25 on Sunday morning.

Two weeks later Tina publicly stated that "The police think he was sold for drugs or to settle a drug debt." She also said she had admitted to the police right away that the adults in the group "shared a marijuana cigarette at the party."

A grand jury was convened to look into the couple's "alleged involvement in crimes including murder, kidnapping, child abuse, and sale of a person," but no indictment was ever brought in. A twenty-three-year-old woman, a close family friend, also became a suspect in this investigation when a pizza delivery boy claimed he saw Randi with her in her apartment two days after the child's disappearance.

Tina Evers later complained that after the party, some of the people who attended it had since lost their jobs because of reports that drug deals took place the night Randi disappeared. "Our good friends are being subpoenaed," she complained bitterly. She was also unhappy when a neighbor gave out her phone number or, as she was quoted as saying, "ratted our number off."

REWARD!

When the Nevada Child Seekers recently raised to $25,000 the small initial reward offered for the return of Randi Evers, his father and stepmother did not appear at the press conference, although they still lived in Las Vegas—not at the same residence, however.

"I'm shocked that they're not here," said Lieutenant Wilbur Jackson, head of the Las Vegas police juvenile detail. "Of course, I've been shocked at their behavior all along," he added.

Patty Giles, executive director of Nevada Child Seekers, says, "Someone at that party knows what happened to that baby, and they probably told others as well. We assume Randi is still alive until we hear otherwise."

REWARD: $26,000
FROM: Nevada Child Seekers, $25,000
Secret Witness, $1,000
FOR: Information leading to Randi Evers's whereabouts and to the arrest and prosecution of the person or persons responsible for his disappearance
CONTACT: Nevada Child Seekers
Telephone: (702) 458-7009

Secret Witness
Telephone: (702) 385-5555

The above information is subject to the warning at the beginning of this book.

REWARD
$50,000

12

Not About
the Kennedys

It was across the road from the home of Ethel Kennedy's brother that one of the most publicized crimes in Connecticut history occurred. In 1975 a nephew of Ethel Kennedy—widow of the late Senator Robert F. Kennedy—was the last person to see a young woman named Martha Moxley alive. Years later, the William Kennedy Smith trial caused a resurgence of interest in any case—especially an unsolved murder—involving any Kennedy relative.

After almost eighteen years, interest in the Moxley murder had died down, but it was revived by Dominick Dunne in his recent novel *A Season in Purgatory*. Dunne admits the novel is based loosely on the murder of Martha Moxley, although he denies it is "about the Kennedys."

This hideous slaying took place on October 30, 1975, the night before Halloween, on the lawn of the

Moxley family's imposing house in the protected Belle Haven section of Greenwich, Connecticut. Even the *New York Times,* which was not given to reporting lurid crimes in 1975, put the story of Martha Moxley on its front page.

The *Times,* along with most other papers in the country, reported the savage attack that occurred sometime between 9:30 P.M. on October 30 and 5:00 A.M. on October 31. That evening Martha had been with teenage classmates from Greenwich High School. They had spent the early hours of that cool October evening playing pranks, part of a Greenwich Halloween tradition called Doorbell Night, or Cabbage Night, when teenagers draped toilet paper from the trees and squirted shaving cream on mailboxes.

According to police reports, the group broke up shortly before 9:30 P.M., leaving Martha sitting in a car parked in the Skakel driveway on Otter Rock Drive. With her were seventeen-year-old Thomas Skakel, his fifteen-year-old brother, Michael, and several other Skakel relatives and friends. A bit later two of the departing teenagers saw Martha and Thomas standing together in the driveway. They reported that they saw "Martha pushing Thomas and Thomas pushing Martha" as they left.

Soon after 9:30 P.M., according to Thomas Skakel, Martha walked to the rear of the Skakel property in the direction of her home, which stood a couple of hundred yards away from the Skakel house.

Martha never reached her front door. Police say she was attacked by someone on the vast lawn of the Moxley property, struck viciously several times with a Ton-

Martha Moxley
Photo courtesy of Dorothy Moxley

ey Penna number six golf iron that investigators later established was owned by the Skakel family.

The force of the beating split the golf club in three places along its tubular shaft. The killer also stabbed Martha five times in the neck with the broken shaft of the club. "Her dungarees had been pulled down," says Connecticut State's Attorney Donald Browne. "There might have been and probably were sexual overtones, although there was never any semen."

Next, Martha's five-foot-five-inch, 120-pound body was probably dragged almost one hundred yards from the front of the Moxley house to the rear of the property. In what police believe was an attempt to conceal the body, her corpse was placed under some willows and pines whose low-hanging branches touched the ground. The killer also hid his weapon, since the section of the shaft that was used to stab Martha was never found.

Thomas Skakel told investigators that on the night of the murder, he had gone back to his room to write a report on Abraham Lincoln for his tenth grade class. According to a recent article in *Greenwich Time*, subsequent questioning of his teachers yielded no information on such an assignment.

A tutor hired to watch over the Skakel boys was also questioned. State's Attorney Browne says, "He [the tutor] has never been cleared or prosecuted. . . . His location during the evening in question has never been . . . documented by other evidence."

In the summer of 1993, the New York *Daily News* reported that investigators for the Skakels were linking the tutor to "unsolved killings of four other girls, and the disappearance of a fifth, in Maine, Massachusetts, and Florida." The incidents occurred when the tutor was living in those areas.

Literally hundreds of people were interviewed. Police looked beyond those immediately present that evening because they could never find a reason for any person who knew Martha to murder her. Well liked by everyone, she had been voted "the girl with the best personality" at her school.

Among the people eyed by investigators—and later cleared—was a twenty-seven-year-old graduate student at Columbia University, who lived in Belle Haven. And the possibility always remained that the murder could have been the work of a transient who wandered into the area from the Connecticut Turnpike or U.S. Route 1.

John Solomon, an investigator for the State's Attorney's Office, says, "We've had a complete reconstruction and complete re-evaluation of all the evidence, re-interviewing many of the witnesses. With all the new forensics available today and not in 1975, we know a hell of a lot more about this case now than we ever did."

But Dorothy Moxley, now a widow, says, "I'm feeling a little panicked because I think the police may be coming to the end of what they can do.

"If they don't solve [the case] now, it's not going to be solved except through public pressure. I don't think whoever killed her wants the publicity. The more it's written about, the more it's talked about, the more it will help."

REWARD: $50,000
FROM: The State of Connecticut, $20,000
The Moxley family, $30,000
FOR: Information leading to the arrest and conviction of those responsible for the death of Martha Moxley
CONTACT: Donald A. Browne, state's attorney for the Judicial District of Fairfield County, Connecticut
Telephone: (203) 579-6506

The above information is subject to the warning at the beginning of this book.

REWARD
$500

13

Lost in the Leather Scene

Whatever Buddy stumbled into that got him killed, it didn't have a thing on earth to do with him being gay," says Jeane McDade of her son, David "Buddy" McDade. A week before his thirtieth birthday, in 1990, Buddy, a hotel employee in San Jose, California, vanished, and his seventy-year-old mother has spent all of her time and money during the last four years trying to find out what happened to him.

Her search has taken her into her son's favorite haunts, the gay "leather bars" of northern California, but she is certain his fate is connected with more than just his unorthodox lifestyle. "The police department would like to make this a gay-bashing-let's-forget-about-it thing," says Mrs. McDade. "They know I don't agree with any of that."

REWARD!

David "Buddy" McDade
Photo courtesy of Jeane McDade

Mrs. McDade thinks Buddy may have been trying to tell her about potential trouble during a phone conversation a week before his June 25, 1990, disappearance. She was vacationing in Scotland at the time and spoke to him "during the wee hours." When she asked how he was doing, he said cryptically, "I'm not going to ruin your vacation. I'll wait until you return."

When Jeane McDade came back to California, she expected Buddy to meet her at the airport in San Francisco, but he wasn't there. When staff from the hotel where he worked called to tell her that Buddy hadn't shown up for a few days, she went into action. After alerting the police, she went right to his apartment, but she had no key and no way to enter.

The Missing Persons Department then supposedly examined the apartment, but they obviously did a less than thorough job. "When I spoke to them one time, they told me my son was black. They weren't very helpful. I don't know whether or not that was because of his lifestyle," she speculates.

Mystified over what had happened to her son, she and her daughter decided to check out the apartment themselves. They put on gloves, went in, and noticed with horror that there were "bloody paper towels." Indeed, there were also blood splotches on the walls "that someone had tried to wash off. Blood all over the ceiling, and one wall looked as though a garden hose had sprayed a fine mist of blood on it." The blood type later turned out to be Buddy's.

But Jeane didn't have to wait for the analysis to come back; as soon as she saw the blood she knew her son was dead. Two years later she had Buddy declared legally dead, even though no body has ever been found.

Jeane McDade says the police forensics specialists are convinced that Buddy was beaten to death. They noted that a chair was missing, and they think he may have been tied to it and beaten and that the killer then destroyed the chair—or took it as a grisly memento.

Adding to the difficulty of finding Buddy, Mrs. McDade has had problems getting information about the case into the papers or on local television. One reporter who tried to help her had to go through six editors. "We finally got a little article in the paper, but it took months," Mrs. McDade says, discouraged. Later she got "America's Most Wanted" to reenact the case, but that has not yet led to any useful clues.

Jeane McDade realized long ago that the only way she would find out anything about Buddy's disappearance was to set off on her own. Armed with photos of her son, she goes to bondage clubs and organizations like SLUG—South Bay Leather Uniform Group. There she circulates among the hairy-chested, tattooed men, some clad only in leather jockstraps, studded belts, or rubber masks. She distributes fliers and talks to anyone who might know anything about Buddy. "Some of them were a little surprised that I was the mother of one of the people there," she says naively. "I guess they don't have a lot of mothers visiting."

Jeane McDade's unconventional odyssey through discipline dens has turned out to be expensive, especially since she tries to cover more than just California. "Last October I tried to send a young man to the National Leather Convention in Chicago, but at the last moment he didn't go." Still, she was able to get fliers distributed there.

Apologetically this mother of three children says she can afford only a $500 reward for information leading to the arrest and conviction of her son's killer. She lives in Santa Cruz, California, on Social Security, is battling cancer, and has spent her life savings on this search. "It's cost me a bundle, everything I have."

As for her son's lifestyle, she says, "I knew he was gay. He had girlfriends, too. He discussed bondage with me," although he didn't tell her that he had actually participated in it. But even if he had, she says, "your children are your children, and none of them are alike. I'm proud of all of them."

REWARD: $500
FROM: Jeane McDade
FOR: Information leading to the arrest and conviction of the murderer of David "Buddy" McDade
CONTACT: District Attorney's Office
County of Santa Clara
San Jose, California
Telephone: (408) 299-7401

The above information is subject to the warning at the beginning of this book.

REWARD
$25,000

14

Angel One!
Code Red!

When Curtis Sliwa emerged from his cold-water flat in the East Village near Tompkins Square Park in New York City on April 23, 1992, for his 5:30 A.M. radio broadcast, he noticed a "darkish gray car, with dirty windows and some long-haired freakazoids inside it" parked nearby. Then he heard loud footsteps and realized "I'm gonna get whumped!" At that moment a bat cracked open the back of his skull.

About two months later, on June 19, he was attacked a second time. On that occasion, the thirty-eight-year-old founder of the Guardian Angels found himself lying in an intensive care unit with "my bowels, intestines, bladder, all blown out, my stomach hanging up like a bag, tubes jammed up my nose, bells ringing every time I took a breath, unable to speak or communicate."

REWARD!

Chief Red Beret Sliwa has always sought out trouble—and vice versa. In 1972 he helped rescue people from a burning building while he was on his newspaper route. Later, as a McDonald's manager who saw the dangers of city life firsthand, he persuaded a group of co-workers to join him in forming what he called the Magnificent Thirteen. This was an early version of the Guardian Angels, the famous, sometimes infamous, citizens' patrol organization, which now has seven thousand unarmed members wearing red berets in forty active chapters in major cities in the United States and in seven cities overseas.

Curtis Sliwa also has a second career as a talk show host. In the midst of the John Gotti trial, Curtis used his new radio forum on WABC as a "bully pulpit" for a daily update on the "Teflon Don," complete with music from the movie *The Godfather.*

Curtis admits that "being part Italian-American and being known as a crime fighter, there was nothing that bothered me more than the young people putting these mobsters—Gambino, Castellano, Gotti—in heroic proportions."

He therefore decided to go on the warpath against them during his dialogues on the radio. "Calls started coming after the shows," he said, "threats that seemed organized and not just the Looney-Tunes and the fringe knuckleheads who would call at the drop of a hat."

All of which probably resulted in his first trouncing in April. On that occasion, as Sliwa fell to his knees and flailed his arms against several attackers wielding bats, a passing cab stopped and gave him a chance to

REWARD!

Curtis and Lisa Sliwa
Photo courtesy of Curtis Sliwa

call for help on his Motorola radio while his attackers jumped in their car and "beat it, 'Untouchables' style, heading north on Avenue A," he says.

The next morning, Curtis was back on the air acting like Superman, bad-mouthing his attackers, and refusing to take precautions. His wife, Lisa, cautioned him, "'Better travel with an entourage.' Even the cops warned me, 'Hey, you're living a charmed life, Sliwa. We may not know who did this. But it certainly isn't your junkie-gonna-blackjack-you-on-the-head-take-your-money routine.'"

Sliwa made more anti-Mafia statements on another television program, and on June 19, when a taxi picked him up near his apartment he found himself looking down the barrel of a "long-nosed thirty-eight" held by a gunman wearing a mask adorned with horses and other animals; the attacker's "butt was wedged against the dashboard" on the passenger side of the front seat; the meter and the plastic partition had been removed, and the rear doors and windows were locked.

It was "the real deal," says Curtis. He thinks that five bullets were fired; one entered his stomach, one hit his legs, and at least one hit his back. In a move that seems incredible, Curtis managed to exit the cab through the open front passenger window and radio for help: "Angel One! Code Red!" Then he collapsed out on the street.

This second attack did more than just jolt Curtis's body. Once he was shot, he realized that it was inevitable that someone would finally reveal what he had tried for so long to hide: that he had made up some early incidents of the Guardian Angels' activities. "I manufactured 'em, I contrived 'em, I'm responsible. So it's about time that we got the record clean. I'll admit I felt I had to be devious in the beginning to get my message across.

"Now I'm sure everyone looks at anything I say or do with a jaundiced eye," he says ruefully. An unfortunate by-product of the timing of his revelations was that "it certainly gave some of my critics in the police department an opportunity to say I made up the attack. But five bullets? Come on!"

The police say that Curtis has never positively iden-

REWARD!

tified anyone as the gunman, although he has his suspicions. And despite the physical and verbal attacks against Curtis Sliwa, he is still out there with his men.

REWARD: $25,000
FROM: Capital Cities Communications (owner of WABC Radio) and individuals, including Congressman Charles Rangel and Private Investigator Bo Dietl
FOR: Information leading to the arrest and conviction of the person who shot Curtis Sliwa
CONTACT: Detective Larry Riccio
9th Precinct, New York
Telephone: (212) 477-7809

The above information is subject to the warning at the beginning of this book.

REWARD
$10,000

15

Stolen by Bikers

Susan Billig of Coconut Grove, Florida, has a terrible story to tell about what she thinks happened to her daughter, Amy, who disappeared in 1974. "She's probably been bought and sold. These bikers sell women to each other," she says with a sigh. "Maybe she's been beaten up around her head and doesn't know where she is or who she is. One biker who tried to help me find her was beaten up and left for dead. Before that, he said, he had purchased my daughter from another biker and my daughter was in such a bad way she didn't even know her name."

For two decades this mother has immersed herself in the dangerous and clandestine world of the outlaw bikers, desperately trying to find out the truth about her daughter. Attending biker rallies, visiting biker clubhouses, and traveling to prisons and seedy outlaw bars no longer seems strange to her.

"I can reach the bikers better than the police because all the bikers have mothers, too. I say to them, 'There's no police involved. I just want to find my child.' They think you're nuts, but they help you. To them I'm that crazy lady from Coconut Grove."

She points out that "these bikers are not what you saw in *The Wild Bunch*. These people have no feelings. I'm not talking about the yuppies in their black leather jackets trying to emulate the bikers. I'm talking about outlaw motorcycle groups.

"The Fort Lauderdale police have some of these people in jail for crimes like nailing a girl to a tree for doing something like wearing colors which are special to them. They don't care at all about people," she said.

It has been twenty years since her daughter, Amy, may have been dragged into this world, years in which her mother went from her forties to her sixties. Recently Susan Billig lost her husband, and now she has cancer and heart problems. But nothing hurt this mother's heart as much as losing her daughter on an otherwise ordinary spring day, March 4, 1974, the day that a caravan of bikers came roaring through town.

"My husband and I received good information later that the bikers had taken Amy," states her mother. "The bikers had been gathering for their yearly run from Daytona Beach, and people said they saw the motorcyclists driving three and four abreast. I think someone asked Amy if she needed a lift. She got on one of their bikes, and she was never able to get off."

The daughter she is looking for, with shoulder-length hair, a buoyant manner, and a loping gait, was special to Sue from the beginning. Amy was her first child,

REWARD!

Amy Billig at age seventeen in 1974
Photo courtesy of Susan Billig

arriving after four miscarriages. After waiting all those years for her, it was even harder to wait the twelve paralyzing days following Amy's disappearance before Sue Billig got her first clue as to where her daughter was.

"We got a tip by telephone that she had been abducted by a motorcycle gang," she says simply. The mystery deepened when Amy's camera was found two days later near the Florida Turnpike. When the film inside it was developed, one of the photos showed a vine-covered building with a white brick house in the background. The vine was not native to Florida, and the building was unfamiliar to the Billigs.

REWARD!

The Billigs connected with two members of the motorcycle gang who had gone through town the day Amy disappeared. Initially they promised to help locate Amy, but then they mysteriously reneged on their promise, calling back two days later to say it would be best if the Billigs forgot about trying to find their daughter.

Fat chance. In the next decade and a half, Sue haunted the biker underworld in search of any trace of Amy. She scoured the back alleys and dives of southern Florida for clues. She searched through filthy clubhouses, met callous biker leaders, even went to the annual biker races at Daytona in the slim hope that her daughter might be there.

One time she found a biker who claimed to have once "owned" Amy in Orlando. He promised to meet Sue there; then he vanished, reappearing eventually with the news that Amy was in Seattle. That led to a week in the Northwest for Sue, during which she combed the dangerous biker dens and seedy topless dives for news of her daughter.

Sue's hegira was beautifully written up by Edna Buchanan in *The Corpse Had a Familiar Face*. "Susan Billig's obsession is more than a story to me," Buchanan admitted. "I too dream about Amy coming home."

That seems unlikely, however, and the longer Amy is away from home, the more apprehensive her mother is about her daughter's fate. During her sorties into the subterranean biker culture, Sue Billig learned that young girls like Amy are often treated like chattels. Bikers trade one girl for another or for money or even

73

REWARD!

for a bike, and all the while the girls are subjected to casual violence and given various drugs.

If Amy is still alive, Sue believes she may have become completely a part of the brutal world surrounding her. "I think she became one with her abductors in order to keep alive."

Sue might not even recognize Amy today should she manage to come home. In all probability Amy would be almost unrecognizable after what she's been through. Her horrific experiences have probably completely removed all traces of the spirited, engaging young girl who left her happy youth behind on that idyllic March afternoon twenty years ago.

REWARD: $10,000
FOR: Information leading to finding Amy Billig dead or alive
CONTACT: Susan Billig
　　　　　　3595 Avocado Ave.
　　　　　　Coconut Grove, FL 33133

The above information is subject to the warning at the beginning of this book.

REWARD
$10,000

—————— 16

The Zodiac Killer, New York Style

It was probably one of the most bizarre series of shootings ever to take place in New York, far stranger certainly than the California Zodiac case, with which it's occasionally confused. And while it was happening, New Yorkers were as fascinated as they were terrified. Once the story broke that someone was stalking and shooting men who had the astrological signs the gunman had chosen in advance, residents were wary of disclosing their birthday to anyone. Even the innocuous come-on line used in singles bars, "What sign are you?" could no longer be asked.

So far, no one knows how the Zodiac killer knew in advance the astrological signs of the four people he shot—one of whom later died. Michael Ciravolo, who was then head of New York's Crimes Against Senior Citizens Squad, says that at the time, "we drew up a

75

profile of the victims. Where did they get their prescription drugs? Were they on welfare? Where did they get their hair cut? Where did they get their eyeglass prescriptions made? For everything that a normal male does we made up lists. The victims had *nothing* in common.

"But *he* knew," says Ciravolo, now president of Superior Investigations & Security in Smithtown, Long Island. "He was never wrong." In only one instance is it believed that the killer directly asked the victim when he was born. Ciravolo says that "in the middle of June 1990, a few days before the thirty-year-old homeless man was shot in Central Park at four o'clock in the morning, the victim remembered that he casually met someone [in that area] who asked him when he was born. But in the rest of the cases no one knew how the Zodiac knew."

Although all of the Zodiac's victims had different signs, many of his shootings had similar features. All took place early on a Thursday morning. The attacks were twenty-one days apart, except for one that occurred sixty-three days after the previous one—but sixty-three is three times twenty-one.

In addition, all the men who were shot were weak-looking or homeless. "All of the victims were in some way defenseless," says Ciravolo. "Two of them walked with canes. One of them was senile. That victim got days and nights mixed up and picked up newspapers from the garbage. Another victim was passed out from drinking when he was shot. Two were homeless, and one of them was sleeping on a park bench when the Zodiac attacked him."

REWARD!

**Sketch of man wanted for questioning in
connection with New York's Zodiac killer**
Sketch courtesy of the New York City Police Department

This nocturnal shooter also wrote taunting notes concerning some of his attacks. In one, he threatened to kill one person for each sign of the Zodiac. That note included ominous phrases like "Zodiac—Time to Die."

The Zodiac shot all of his victims in the back. "For example," Ciravolo says, "the seventy-eight-year-old victim who was shot on May 31, 1990, was asked by the Zodiac for a drink of water, and when he didn't reply and kept walking, the Zodiac shot him from the rear."

REWARD!

The Zodiac also terrified at least one victim after shooting him. A fifty-year-old man walking with a cane saw someone wearing a brown ski mask and gloves. The man crossed the street to meet him. The Zodiac put a gun against his back and shot him in the spine. As the victim lay bleeding, the assailant reached down, held the gun to the terrified man's face for a moment or two, and then ran off.

Five times during the summer and fall of 1990, undercover police officers patrolled certain areas, hobbling along on sticks and canes on "astrologically propitious" nights twenty-one days apart when the Zodiac was likely to strike again. But "Operation Watchdog had become Operation Chihuahua," says Mike Pearl of the *New York Post,* for the killer did not strike again.

Like the California Zodiac killer a decade before, New York's Zodiac killer simply vanished. All that is known of him, from his notes and from his comments to the survivors, is that he is a Taurus with family troubles. A black man with a dark complexion, he's thirty to thirty-five years old, six feet tall, 180 pounds, with a receding hairline, a short Afro, a mustache, and possibly a beard. He wore a black bracelet on his left wrist during one of his attacks.

His notes showed him to be educated, with a knowledge of French and Latin. He is also familiar with astrology and ballistics. And one last thing: while he was living in New York—he may since have moved— he enjoyed walking in Central Park at night. Proof enough that he was crazy, some think.

REWARD!

REWARD: $10,000
FROM: The Office of the Mayor of the City of New York
FOR: Information leading to the conviction of the gunman known as the Zodiac killer
CONTACT: New York City Police Chief of Detectives
Telephone: (212) 374-5430
or Queens Homicide
Telephone: (718) 520-9255

The above information is subject to the warning at the beginning of this book.

REWARD
$1,000

The Prophet of Profits

She could be wandering with a mental problem. She could be a suicide. Or she could be a homicide," says Jim Barratt, the distraught father of missing forty-one-year-old Brenda Barratt Kerber, who joined a cult—and disappeared.

His daughter's identification papers were found in the pocketbook she left behind, but her car was missing. Her house showed no sign of disarray, although the police have not ruled out the possibility of foul play.

All that is known about Brenda's last few months is that she became a follower of a New Age guru known as Rama, whose real names is Frederick P. Lenz III. After her disappearance, Brenda's parents learned a lot about this California Raisin Cult, as it's sometimes called, and what they learned did nothing to calm their concern about her state of mind before she disappeared.

Says Barratt, a Corvallis, Oregon, travel agent, who was once the director of athletics at Oregon State University, "We are very bitter with this Zen Buddhist group that recruited her from a normal life."

The fast-food meditation philosophy that attracted Brenda has made a lot of other parents unhappy as well. "We have consistently received complaints about Rama over the past two or three years," says Cynthia Kisser, executive director of the Chicago-based Cult Awareness Network.

Lenz—sometimes called the Yuppie Guru because his father was the mayor of Stamford, Connecticut, in

Brenda Barratt Kerber as a teenager
Photo courtesy of James G. Barratt

the early 1970s—looks like a cross between Elayne Boosler and Richard Simmons. He's known to the public mostly from the poster for his meditation workshops. In it, he is seated in the lotus position, with a startling shock of luminous hair, created by heavy backlighting. The other familiar advertisement for his organization shows a woman meditating on a Porsche. Not so odd as it sounds: *Newsday* reported that Lenz owned two Porsches, two Range Rovers, and three Mercedes-Benzes!

The one thing no one questions is that Lenz's goal is to make money. He gathers his disciples together for seminars designed to help them get jobs in the field of computer science. And the more money they make, the more they turn over to the coffers of the cult.

Although Lenz's followers often live in poverty, members and outsiders who take the workshops— which now rarely make any mention of Rama, or Lenz, probably because of all the bad publicity—are allowed to pay with credit cards. At one time, only one-hundred-dollar bills were accepted by this group; anything smaller was considered "low-vibed."

The pressure to come up with the money and conform to the group is overwhelming. "Before Brenda disappeared, she had taken out a six-thousand-dollar loan to enroll in their programming course," her parents say. "She had no prior training in this kind of work, and she couldn't do it."

When Brenda lost her computer job after two months at Orion Films, she was inconsolable. "It's a losing battle," she wrote in one of the diaries that were found in her apartment after she disappeared. "Getting a job . . . and having enough money to pay my seminar fees."

Without the money, she also got no sympathy. In her diary she wrote that she had approached Rama, who professes to have been an English professor in his previous incarnation and is now, according to his own modest assessment, one of twelve truly enlightened beings on the planet. He may be enlightened, but he doesn't appear to be compassionate. When Brenda told him she didn't have money, she wrote that "he was very stern and impersonal with me."

Before she joined the group, Brenda had been despondent over her divorce from her childhood sweetheart. She perked up after she joined Lenz's cult, however, and even gave up custody of her adored son to go and study with Lenz. But before she disappeared on September 28, 1989, she had again become increasingly depressed and withdrawn.

When last seen, Brenda Kerber weighed 130 pounds; she is five feet three inches tall with brown hair and hazel eyes. Her car, a 1982 tan Ford Granada station wagon, New York license plate number TXU-294, has never been found.

REWARD: $1,000
FROM: Jim Barratt
FOR: Information leading to the whereabouts of Brenda Kerber
CONTACT: Detectives John Kellerher or Al Cuzzo
White Plains, New York, Police Department
Telephone: (914) 422-6111

The above information is subject to the warning at the beginning of this book.

REWARD
$200,000 to
$250,000 (Canadian
dollars)

18

Three Canadian Children

Alison Parrott, Nicole Morin, and Michael Dunahee all disappeared in Canada. Each case has a gigantic reward, and in all three situations, someone has spent an enormous amount of time and effort trying to find them and their abductors or killers—but to no avail.

Alison Parrott

One wouldn't have expected Alison Parrott to be in this group of missing children because she had just completed a "streetproofing" seminar designed to teach children how to protect themselves from harm. She'd learned to keep her distance when talking to someone she didn't know, to stand back if someone in a car stopped and asked for directions, never to tell a telephone caller there was no one else at home, and more.

But no one ever warned her about "photographers." Someone should have because, according to Detective Stephen Irwin of the Metropolitan Toronto Police Force Sexual Assault Squad, a phony photographer act "is something that is used with all age groups, even by serial offenders. Holding a camera is a way to get people's attention and get their guard down. It helps start a conversation and personalizes it. Often there's not even any film in the camera."

Had Alison known this, however, it might still not have helped her. As her mother, advertising executive Lesley Parrott, says, "You can do everything in your power to give your children the information they need to protect themselves. But ultimately, if you get a devious adult up against an eleven-year-old child, there's no competition."

Alison's abductor was not only devious, he was determined. He singled out this mature-looking child, whom he probably first saw at a track meet, and then called all the Parrotts in the Toronto phone book until he found her.

When he spoke to her on July 25, 1986, he said he wanted to photograph her, along with some other players from her school, for a track magazine. Alison called her mother, who allowed her daughter to meet the mysterious man, since it would be in a public place at a major intersection, at the northwest corner of the Varsity Stadium at Bedford and Bloor.

Two days later Alison was found in Kingsmill Park, murdered, with evidence of sexual assault. Although people all over Toronto claimed to have seen her in various places around that time, Detective Irwin explained how people's recollections can easily be influenced in any investigation. For example, "An investigator says to them, 'What shade of blue was the car?' And even though in the back of their minds they thought it was black or gray, they think the policeman must know and they start thinking the car was blue. Thousands of posters of Alison Parrott were distributed and pinned up, so what people think they saw could have meshed with what they actually saw in the posters."

Detective Irwin, who has been working on this case for eight years, "has been particularly passionate about it," according to Lesley Parrott. "His own father, a policeman, was murdered on duty, so that gives Stephen Irwin a special concern. He told me that every time he goes by the cemetery, there are two people he thinks of: his father and Alison. And every July twenty-fifth he'll phone me up," knowing that has to be a difficult day for her.

Actually, all days are difficult for this forty-six-year-old advertising executive. "I never go to bed at night or get up in the morning without immediately thinking of Alison. But I still have a great deal of difficulty recalling the happy memories. The pain of her death makes it very hard for me to have the pleasure of recalling the incredibly joyous life we had together."

There is one big question, of course: who did it? All that is known is that at least once the killer used a photography ruse to get his victim. "Did the person continue to do this afterward?" asks Detective Irwin. "Did he set out initially to murder this girl, or was he a potential sex offender who used the phone all the

Alison Parrott
Photo courtesy of Lesley C. Parrott

time but never found anyone who would meet him? And finally when he does, did he end up in a position where he does something and feels very guilty and fears this victim can identify him and out of self-preservation commits the murder? Any time there's a photographer situation it comes across my desk, yet we haven't had the luck to resolve this one."

Lesley Parrott adds a last warning note. "One of the things about this case is that we are an ordinary middle-class family, not rich, not poor. We weren't living in the 'wrong part of town.' My husband and I both have good professions, and we were two immigrants who made good. We always put our kids first. We taught Alison to be careful, and she was a child who obeyed the rules. If this can happen to us, it can happen to anybody."

Nicole Morin

"Concerned citizen, a heinous crime has been committed—not only against the Morin family but against our society!" That is how the reward poster for little Nicole Morin reads. In this case, it is the father who is obsessed, still searching for his daughter who was nine years old when she disappeared somewhere between the twentieth floor and the lobby of her apartment building, after leaving her home to take the elevator downstairs.

"She was never actually seen entering the elevator," says her father, fifty-three-year-old Art Morin. "She left our condo [the West Mall in Etobicoke near Toronto], and whether she entered the elevator or not, nobody knows."

At the time, Art Morin and his wife were separated, and Nicole, who was living with her mother, was on her way to meet a friend in the lobby so the two could go to the pool together. When Nicole failed to show up in the lobby around eleven o'clock, the friend called up through the intercom, Morin says, "and asked, 'Isn't Nicole coming down?' And my wife thought, 'Well, she must be on her way.'"

Jeanette Morin, fifty-seven, speaks rapidly with a heavy French accent. "It was around three o'clock in

REWARD!

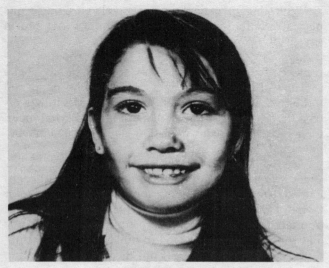

Nicole Morin
Photo prepared by Child Find, courtesy of Metropolitan Toronto Police

the afternoon when I realized something was going on. I just became in a daze. I kept saying, 'Oh, she's got to be with somebody playing and she forgot.' Around six o'clock, I couldn't put up with it anymore. I called the cops."

Jeanette believes, "There's a possibility that Nicole is alive. She could be in the States. . . . I don't give up hope." Neither does Art Morin, who worked with a private investigator for three years, with the help of funds raised by the community, looking for his daughter, who would now be seventeen.

REWARD!

"With this investigator, we traveled to numerous places, but there was nothing concrete," Art Morin says sadly. "We exhausted everything."

Says Sergeant Rick Rolfe of the Metropolitan Toronto Police Department, "This appears to have been a crime of opportunity by a predator who happened to be in that building at that time." Art Morin has his own theories. "If she was abducted by a sex offender, then most likely she died that day. But I don't believe that."

Meanwhile, he can't stop searching for her. "A few years ago I got a report that there was a little girl named Nicole Morin going to school on Vancouver Island. I flew out immediately to identify this little girl. You talk about being nervous! But it wasn't her. It was an awful letdown. You kind of build up your expectations, and it just goes right out the window. You kind of get depressed afterward."

Quite recently he heard that a Nicole Morin was in the studio audience of a game show someone saw in the States. He tracked down the program—but again the girl wasn't his daughter. "You've got to check everything," he says. "There's always the chance someone will have a knock of conscience and recall something."

When she disappeared, Nicole was four feet four inches tall, weighed 60 pounds, had a medium complexion, petite build, and slightly protruding uneven teeth with a center gap. She was last seen wearing a salmon-colored one-piece bathing suit.

REWARD!

Michael Dunahee

The Dunahees have dedicated their lives to finding out what happened to their son, even putting together a search center in their basement. Says Bruce Dunahee of his five-year-old son, "You could spot his eyes fifty feet away." Michael was also extremely small and Bruce thinks, "Maybe somebody wanted a young child and since he looked so young, they took him."

Whoever took Michael had to have worked very fast, snatching him in under five minutes from a playground at the Blanchard Street Elementary School on King Street in Victoria, British Columbia, a few minutes away from the famous Empress Hotel.

On March 24, 1991, Bruce and his wife, Crystal, were in the parking lot when Michael asked to play in the playground next door. The parents looked over and saw a couple of other kids there and said yes. It was 12:35 P.M. For the next five minutes they pushed their six-month-old daughter in her baby carriage, while Michael, wearing multicolored sweat pants and short-sleeved T-shirt bearing a picture of Ninja Turtles surfing, went off to play by himself.

"The field was only about fifty feet away, and it was out of our view for less than five minutes. When I turned around, I didn't see Michael or the other children," says the distraught father.

Later, when the other kids who had been playing there were tracked down, a few said they had seen a brown van with a dog in a cage in the back. "They didn't know what breed it was, but it was sort of a coffee-table-size dog. But we can't be sure if that had

REWARD!

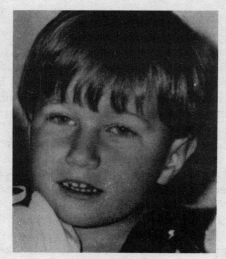

Michael Dunahee
Photo courtesy of Bruce Dunahee

anything to do with what happened to Michael," his father says of their three-foot tall, 45-pound child with sandy blond hair and a smattering of freckles.

"The police still don't know whether he was picked up by a pedophile or whether it was an 'adoption' or pornography ring, or worse. The only thing they have ruled out completely is a satanic cult."

The police have also ruled out the possibility that Michael is still in Victoria. "We're on an island, and there are ferries and he could have been taken north or he could have ended up in the United States," Bruce Dunahee says.

REWARD!

Wherever he is, "a big part of our life is missing right now, and we can't have any more kids," says the obsessed thirty-one-year-old father. He and his wife, who have known each other since they were six years old, work with the help of forty to fifty volunteers to find Michael. "The only work I've been able to do since he disappeared is to run my search center in the basement," says Dunahee.

The search center "does up address labels and wanted circulars and sends them to police stations all over North America . . . as well as to bus lines and trains, doctors and dentists, and day care and schools. We've probably mailed out two and a half million posters ourselves, and we're registered with about a hundred missing-children organizations in Canada, North America, and Europe."

REWARD: $250,000 (Canadian dollars)
FROM: Metropolitan Toronto Police
FOR: Arrest and conviction of the person or persons responsible for the murder of Alison Parrott
CONTACT: Detective Stephen Irwin
                Metropolitan Toronto Police
                Telephone: (416) 324-2222

REWARD: Probably $250,000 (Canadian dollars)*
FROM: Metropolitan Toronto Police
FOR: The arrest and conviction of the person or persons responsible for the abduction of Nicole Morin

*Canadian rewards remain in effect for specified periods of time. This one has expired, but the Metropolitan Toronto Police said the reward would "most likely" be revived if someone came along with the desired information.

REWARD!

C O N T A C T : Metropolitan Toronto Police
Telephone: (416) 324-2222
or Crime Stoppers (if you wish to remain
anonymous)
Telephone: (416) 222-8477

R E W A R D : $200,000 (Canadian dollars)
F R O M : Public donation (in trust)
F O R : The safe return of Michael Dunahee
C O N T A C T : Victoria, British Columbia, Police Department
Telephone: (604) 384-4111
In the United States, call the National Center for
Missing and Exploited Children
Telephone: 1-800-843-5678

The above information is subject to the warning at the beginning of this book.

REWARD
Up to $10,000

19

An Adoptee's Rage

Joe Sinnott was thirteen when he was adopted by Rob and Marcia Edwards, and at eighteen, he was probably the one who murdered them. The Edwardses were found shot to death in rural Pontiac, Illinois. When Rob's employer, a local building contractor, wondered why his usually punctual employee had failed to show up at work, he went to the Edwards home. He was shocked to discover the body of Marcia Edwards, two 9mm automatic gunshot wounds in her face.

Joe's boss walked around the property looking for clues. That's when he happened on Rob's body in the 1979 Lincoln that was kept in a metal utility shed the Edwardses used as a garage. There were two 9mm automatic gunshot wounds in Rob's head as well. No weapon was in sight.

Nor was their adopted son, Joe Sinnott Edwards.

Joe Sinnott had been born in Chicago in 1964. Abandoned by his mother, he had moved through a series of foster homes in Chicago and Bloomington, Illinois. He was such a mischief-maker that he had to be removed from the children's home as well as from a foster home program.

But the Edwardses knew none of this when Joe came into their lives seven years after their marriage. Thirty-five-year-old Rob, a former Green Beret in Vietnam, and Marcia, thirty-three, had married in the hope of having a family, but when they were unable to conceive, they started thinking of adoption.

Detective John Johnson of the Livingston County Sheriff's Department says that when Rob and Marcia went to visit the Salem Children's Home in 1977, "they were looking to adopt a young child. But, due to their age, the adoption agency talked them into adopting an older child." By that time, Rob was forty-two and Marcia was forty.

At first Joe intrigued them. This sad but compelling-looking boy with big eyes looked as if he needed a lot of love. That was what the Edwards wanted to give. Since they lived near Salem, the home let Joe stay with them for a while. According to Detective Johnson, "Joe was on pretty good behavior while he was first with them. It was only after the adoption that he began displaying his severe behavioral problems."

It seems that the new son of the warm and loving Edwardses was into alcohol, glue-sniffing, and drugs. They also had to contend with discipline problems at school, the vandalization of a house, as well as suicide

REWARD!

1980 photo and 1988 sketch of Joe Sinnott Edwards
Courtesy of Livingston County Sheriff's Police, Pontiac, Illinois

attempts and other crises that punctuated the two years that Joe actually lived with them.

Finally Joe began to threaten them. This sometimes happened when they wouldn't give him what he wanted; at other times there was no apparent reason for it. As a result, the Edwardses began to look over their shoulders nervously when their son was around during the day. And the frightened couple started to lock themselves into their own bedroom at night.

Fearing that all they had worked for would end up in Joe's unstable hands after their death, they rewrote their wills, specifically stating they were omitting him for "personal reasons" and because "he is not in a position to accept financial responsibilities."

REWARD!

In 1979, when Joe was fifteen, he was sent to the Minot, North Dakota, Boys Ranch, but they were unable to cope with him and returned him to the Edwards home in October 1980. Thereafter Joe was supposed to have left for a trade school in Florida, but witnesses reported seeing him in Ann Arbor, Michigan. They said that Joe had a 9mm automatic gun with him and that he was talking about killing his adoptive parents. Then he dropped out of sight for a year and a half, no doubt to the immense relief of Rob and Marcia Edwards.

On January 19, 1983, however, Joe was spotted in the town of Pontiac. Two days later his adoptive parents, Rob and Marcia Edwards, who had so magnanimously taken this boy into their home and spent so much money trying to save him, were found dead.

Although warrants were issued against Joe after the murders, the fact that he had never been fingerprinted made it hard to find him.

Detective Johnson says it is probably unlikely that Joe knew he had been cut out of his adoptive parents' substantial estate. He added, "it would be a strong presumption" that Joe may have been in trouble with the law since the murder of Rob and Marcia. "He could have been in jail or in prison, possibly under one of his aliases," which include José Sinnott, Joseph Wenzlaff, and Joseph Wickam.

Johnson says Joe is suicidal and a known drug user. He is five feet ten inches tall, weighs 165 pounds, has blue-gray or hazel eyes and dark brown hair. There is a small tattoo of a cross on his left hand between the

REWARD!

thumb and index finger. He should be considered extremely dangerous.

Unfortunately Rob and Marcia Edwards didn't realize that until it was too late.

REWARD: Up to $10,000
FROM: A reward trust
FOR: Information leading to the arrest and conviction of Joe Sinnott Edwards
CONTACT: Livingston County Sheriff's Police
Pontiac, Illinois
Telephone: (815) 844-7171

The above information is subject to the warning at the beginning of this book.

REWARD
$1,000

20

Murder on Music Row

Country music superstars Kris Kristofferson and Willie Nelson were recording nearby, and Dolly Parton's cousin, Cindy Parton, found the body. Nashville performers Alan Smith, Jimmy Payne, and Steve Bivins sang spirituals at the memorial service, and big names guaranteed big headlines for this story. But the massive investigation spawned by public interest has failed to solve the case.

Public interest in the murder of Kevin Hughes is still strong in Nashville. "Even though this killing occurred in a high crime area, and it could have been a street robbery gone bad, rumors that it was connected to the music industry continue to swirl," says Rob Moritz, a reporter for the Nashville *Banner*. Whatever the reason for the shooting, the result was that Hughes was shot to death in downtown Nashville's Music Row district shortly after ten o'clock on the night of March 10, 1989.

Hughes, age twenty-three, the bearded heavyset country music chart director of *Cash Box* magazine, and Sammy Sadler, an Evergreen Records recording artist and aspiring country singer, who was also overweight and had a beard, had just eaten at a local seafood restaurant. After dinner they returned to Sadler's place of business, the Evergreen Records office at 1021 Sixteenth Avenue South, to make some phone calls.

At one point, they heard the locked street door of the building rattling. Hughes went to the door to check it out. There he saw someone, a black man, wearing what he thought was a ski cap. When he returned, he told Sammy about it. Unconcerned, the two left the building fifteen or twenty minutes later.

Detective Bill Pridemore of the Nashville Metro Police Murder Squad says they walked to Kevin's car, which was parked directly across the street. They opened the doors of Kevin's blue Pontiac and were preparing to slide in when someone approached Sadler on the passenger side. Suddenly the sound of gunfire exploded in the quiet street. Sammy Sadler looked down and saw that he had been shot in the shoulder. As he fled for cover, he yelled out to his friend, who was still outside the car: "Run, Kevin! Run!" Then Sadler ducked into a nearby apartment building.

As Kevin Hughes tried to bolt, the gunman swiftly fired four more shots. Hughes took three hits, including one at close range in the face. He died soon after in a pool of his own blood. Cindy Parton later told the Nashville *Banner,* "There was blood all over. Blood

REWARD!

Kevin Hughes
Photo courtesy of Barbara and Larry Hughes

gushing from his face left a three-foot trail on the road."

People described the suspect as anywhere from 170 to 215 pounds in weight, and about five feet nine inches in height. Most said he wore a mask. His hat fell off during the attack or when he ran away, and it remains a major clue. On the royal blue baseball cap were the words "World War II Veteran and Damn Proud of It."

Kevin Hughes of Carmi, Illinois, was a trumpet player who loved music so much that when he was young he used to persuade his family to drive forty miles just to buy music magazines. He enrolled in

REWARD!

Nashville's Belmont College in 1983 to learn about the music business. At the time of his death, he had not yet graduated, but he was working for *Cash Box,* the music trade publication. There he helped compile the weekly country music charts, regularly calling one hundred radio stations around the country for the information he needed.

Information is what the police need now. Instead, they've been getting rumors and speculation, all of which have been checked out by detectives Pat Postiglione and Bill Pridemore. One theory they've discarded was that it wasn't *Cash Box* employee Hughes but Sammy Sadler who was the actual target. "But if Sammy was the target," says Detective Pridemore, "why go after Kevin and chase him down the street and risk being hit by cars and seen by other people?"

Kevin Hughes's mother, Barbara, is still trying to cope with the mystery of her son's death. She discounts a robbery motive. "There was nothing taken," she says as she tries to come up with some other plausible explanation. But there is none. "There's no logic out there. I'm looking for some kind of reason. It's all so senseless. But I believe, as others do, that it [the murder] was connected to the music business in some way."

Music chart tampering—and whether Hughes did or did not cooperate in such an undertaking—underlies the theory that the music business was somehow the cause of the slaying. "There's a lot of people in the music business," says Detective Pridemore. "People in that business always want to eliminate their competition."

REWARD!

But maybe it isn't just competition and paranoia and a desire to eradicate the enemy. On several occasions Hughes had noticed when the magazine was printed that the charts he had created had been modified by others. He had also confided to friends that he had been asked several times to manipulate the charts in return for money. He told his friends he had always refused. And a week or so before his slaying, he had received threats that left him worried.

Was he about to reveal what he was being pressured to do? Or was he already doing something illegal? In a significant, if cryptic, comment on the phone only two days before his murder, Hughes told his friend Mike McMillan that "he didn't like what he had become."

McMillan will never forget that Hughes told him he couldn't talk at that point because he was calling from the office. "He [Kevin] told me he'd tell me everything on Saturday, his day off. Of course, that day never came."

REWARD: $1,000
FROM: Nashville Crimestoppers
FOR: Information leading to the arrest and conviction of the killer of Kevin Hughes
CONTACT: Nashville Murder Squad Detectives Bill Pridemore or Pat Postiglione
Telephone: (615) 862-7329

The above information is subject to the warning at the beginning of this book.

21

He Had a Problem with Women

After Larry George's wife, Geraldine, left him, "Larry got out of control," says Detective Tom Bowerman, of the Talladega, Alabama, Police Department. Larry moved into his car "so he could better keep an eye on Geraldine. He followed her to Wal-Mart, where she was a clerk, and he was there when she got off work. He kept calling her, and he had a nephew who worked at Wal-Mart and had him keep an eye on Geraldine as well."

When poor Geraldine was at home, her estranged husband, dressed in his army fatigues, "checked out who was parked near her apartment, copying down tag numbers and descriptions of the cars. A little satellite-dish listening device to eavesdrop on his wife was also later found in his vehicle."

REWARD!

Exasperated and fearful, Geraldine got a warrant out on her former husband. "Larry George was arrested in January of 1988 and the next month the shooting occurred," according to Captain W. E. Hurst of the Talladega Police Department, who went on to tell what happened. "Witnesses say that Larry George confronted Geraldine after she came home one evening," he states. "Larry George often fought with Geraldine over her using a baby-sitter, who was their next-door neighbor, to watch their two little children while she worked at Wal-Mart."

The baby-sitter, Janice Morris, shared her home with Ralph Swain. According to Captain Hurst, when Larry entered their apartment, "He fired one shot and killed Janice immediately.

"Larry George then saw his estranged wife, Geraldine, curled up behind the chair," the captain continues. "He fired one shot into her, paralyzing her from the waist down." The dead baby-sitter's boyfriend, Ralph Swain, "confronted Larry George who then fired one shot into Swain, blowing off the back of his head."

Surprisingly, since the murders, Larry George has come back to the area to see his sister. He has also taken a big risk by going to Wilmington, Delaware, since he surely knows that police have that city under surveillance now that his mother and another sister have moved there.

"We feel he's in and out of Wilmington," says Detective Bowerman. "The last known sighting of Larry George was in Delaware in June of 1990," Bowerman says. "He was calling himself William. He had found

REWARD!

Larry George
Photo courtesy of Talladega, Alabama, Police Department

a girlfriend and showed up at her place every Sunday night.

"Larry George had always loved watching television with Geraldine," says the Alabama detective. "He especially liked to critique the police shows, commenting on how someone could have gotten away with something better."

With this new girlfriend, Larry George also "sat and watched TV. He would come over on Saturday nights, watch TV, shower, and leave the next morning before daylight." Bowerman adds that "this woman wasn't a real class act herself. She was a cocaine addict. They argued over money, and he just quit coming over."

Geraldine refused to be interviewed for this book, indicating it was too painful to go over all the details again. But some time back, her relationship with Larry George and his background was investigated by crime writers Stephen Michaud and Hugh Aynesworth in their book, *Murderers Among Us*. They learned that Larry George was the sole male child in a family of girls. His father, Ransom George, died when he was young, and his mother went blind afterward, possibly as a result of the beatings her husband administered to her.

Larry drifted through the army and a series of jobs like supply clerk. He began to straighten out his life when he married Geraldine, and they had two children. He even purchased a plot of land on which they planned to build a house. But he became abusive, and Geraldine left him. And that's when his deterioration began.

Larry George is six feet two inches tall, weighs 175 to 180 pounds, and is muscular. He was born on December 19, 1955. He smokes mentholated cigarettes and has a conspicuous tattoo on his left biceps: the name Trish with a floral design around it.

"He graduated from truck driving school, and it is possible he may be driving a truck or doing day labor, maybe working around truck stops or off-loading trucks," says Detective Bowerman. "[We know] he's being paid cash because we've done checks on his Social Security and there's no income reported.

"He used to travel with a duffel, keeping his things in plastic bags to protect them from the rain. He was like a pack rat, and everything he needed to survive was in there. He also used to wear military fatigues, but we don't know if he's still doing that."

REWARD!

With or without a duffel or military garb, "we're pretty darned sure wherever he is, he's not going to be far away from his family," says Bowerman. "He was a family-type person, not a criminal-type person. He had no criminal history before he was arrested for harassing Geraldine. We've always felt that his family is our best connection for finding him."

REWARD: $10,000
FROM: Alabama Governor's Office
     Murder Fugitive Program
FOR: The arrest and conviction of Larry George
CONTACT: Talladega, Alabama, Police Department
     Telephone: (205) 362-4508

The above information is subject to the warning at the beginning of this book.

REWARD
$100,000

22

Blown Away in Belle Meade

Aging millionaire David King was a rags-to-riches Russian immigrant who came to the United States in 1912 at the age of fourteen. He started peddling merchandise on foot in Tennessee, eventually opened a hardware store, and then went on into real estate.

On October 29, 1985, an explosion occurred at the home of David King's niece, Melba Lapidus, and her husband, Charles, instantly killing Melba, who was working in the kitchen. The Lapidus home in the Belle Meade section of Nashville was demolished in an explosion so powerful it rocked cars several hundred yards away and so loud it could be heard many blocks from the house.

The husband, Charles, was not injured by the blast. The owner of a women's apparel firm in Nashville, he posted a reward of $100,000 for information about the person who bombed his house and killed his wife. "I have a lot of confidence in law enforcement people," he says. "They were diligent. They have not stopped."

Cummins Beaty of the federal government's Alcohol, Tobacco and Firearms unit told the Nashville *Banner,* "It's a very hard case to work because the force of the detonation destroyed all the evidence. That bomb . . . tore that house to pieces, and it vaporized Melba, more or less."

Interestingly, sixty-three-year-old Melba Lapidus was supposed to be David King's heir, but the day after King wrote a will leaving everything to her and a nephew, he wrote another will leaving everything to a couple he had befriended. However, there has never been any link between the blast and this couple, who later lost their claim on King's money when the second will was ruled invalid. In 1990, David King died mentally incompetent as the result of Alzheimer's disease.

Charles Lapidus says bitterly that his wife's death not only stole the years they could have spent together but also "robbed her of her golden years. The children were grown and educated and settled. We were reasonably affluent. We no longer had college debts and mortgages. We could enjoy life, we were in good health, we were relatively young. All that pleasure was taken away from Melba. She was deprived, not just the rest of us."

REWARD: $100,000
FROM: Charles Lapidus

REWARD!

F O R : Information leading to the arrest and conviction of the killer or killers of Melba Lapidus
C O N T A C T : Nashville Metro Police
Telephone: (615) 862-7400

The above information is subject to the warning at the beginning of this book.

REWARD
$200,000

23

Abductor's Choice

Imagine the horror experienced by eleven-year-old Jacob Wetterling, who was riding his bike home one night with his brother and a friend when suddenly a masked man with a gun jumped into the street and ordered them to throw their bikes into a ditch and lie facedown on the ground.

Jacob, his ten-year-old brother Trevor, and their friend Aaron Larson lay there trembling in terror as they wondered what would happen next. The gunman slowly walked back and forth studying the three boys. Finally he selected one. He roughly snatched Jacob up by the back of his clothing and ordered the other two to go away.

This shocking scene took place in St. Cloud, Minnesota, on October 22, 1989, when the three boys were on their way home from a neighborhood convenience store where they had rented a videotape. After the horrifying experience, Trevor and Aaron ran directly to the Wetterling house. There they alerted a baby-sitter who called her father, the police, and the Wetterlings.

Although firefighters, officers from the sheriff's department, FBI agents, state patrolmen, helicopters, and bloodhounds were rapidly sent to the scene, nothing was ever found except fresh tire tracks, assumed to be from the abductor's vehicle.

Police believe this may have been linked to an earlier sexual assault on a Cold Spring, Minnesota, youth in January of 1989. And there was a nebulous description of the abductor in that case. Detective Ralph Boeckers of the sheriff's department described him as "approximately five feet ten inches tall, wearing a dark ski-type mask or a nylon sock over his head, and gloves. And that's all we have."

Patty and Jerry Wetterling's search for their son led to the posting of a $200,000 reward as well as to the formation of the Jacob Wetterling Foundation to help prevent "stranger abduction of children." This center has amassed some chilling statistics about child abduction in America. For example, in an average year, more than 100,000 *reported* attempted abductions of children occur. Most are unsuccessful attempts by strangers to lure children into automobiles.

Even when not abducted, one in three girls and one in six boys will be sexually abused or victimized before the age of eighteen. Sex offenders who attack young boys molest an average of 281 boys in a lifetime. In the majority of cases, the victim and offender know

REWARD!

Jacob Wetterling
Photo courtesy of the Jacob Wetterling Foundation

each other at least casually, and half the time physical force is used. Perhaps most chilling, "child sex offenders are rarely apprehended and convicted for the most serious charges," probably because most victims are afraid and unwilling to talk about what transpired.

Of course, none of this information sheds light on what happened to blue-eyed Jacob Wetterling, who probably faced an even more frightening ordeal after the kidnapper grabbed him. Three weeks after his abduction, Jacob's parents told an interviewer that either they could believe that Jacob was fine and would one day come home or they could try not to think about any of the horrible things that could have happened to him. They have chosen to believe that one day he'll be home.

R E W A R D : $200,000
F O R : The safe return of Jacob Wetterling
C O N T A C T : Jacob Wetterling Foundation
                    Telephone: 1-800-325-HOPE

The above information is subject to the warning at the beginning of this book.

REWARD
$25,000

24

"Frug" Is a Four-Letter Word

Forty-nine-year-old Mary Joe Frug went out on the evening of April 4, 1991, to buy cookies at a grocery store in her hometown of Cambridge, Massachusetts. She lived in a safe neighborhood; elegant Victorian and Tudor mansions and oversized contemporary residences faced out onto the quiet tree-lined street.

Someone—perhaps the male seen running down a nearby road just before her body was found—forever shattered the safety of the neighborhood by plunging a seven-inch military knife five times into her chest and thighs in what was obviously a violent sexual assault.

Later, in the darkness of that night, Mary Joe Frug was found on the street, dying in a pool of blood. By the time she was brought to Mount Auburn Hospital a few blocks away from Sparks Street where the attack occurred, she was already dead.

Mary Joe Frug would have been just another one of the increasing number of murder victims in Massachusetts, except that she was a professor at the New England School of Law and her husband was a professor at Harvard Law School. Furthermore, because of a controversy over a parody of her liberal use of four-letter words, her death became the focus of quite a brouhaha.

Mary Joe Frug
Photo courtesy of Hutchins Photography,
Watertown, Massachusetts

REWARD!

To greatly oversimplify the events that occurred after Mary Joe Frug's death, some students created a parody of Frug's feminist writings, using Frug's own inimitable writing style. Frug occasionally used language academia was unaccustomed to seeing in scholarly papers. For example, *Vanity Fair* quoted her as having written: "not all pornography is simply about women being fucked. There are some pornographic works in which women fuck."

Students angrily took sides concerning the spoof. Feminists accused those who had parodied Frug's writings of conducting "a necrophiliac gang bang upon the living body of her work." Even the faculty got involved, including Alan Dershowitz and Lawrence Tribe.

Today the subject of Mary Joe Frug is still such a touchy one that it's hard to get a statement about her from the New England School of Law or the Middlesex County D.A.'s office. The school did provide a photograph and a statement saying they were offering a reward of $25,000 for the conviction of the person who murdered her.

REWARD: $25,000
FROM: New England School of Law
FOR: Information resulting in the arrest and conviction of the person or persons who murdered Professor Mary Joe Frug
CONTACT: Office of Middlesex County District Attorney
Thomas Reilly
Telephone: (617) 494-4050

The above information is subject to the warning at the beginning of this book.

REWARD
$10,000

25

Missing on the Redneck Riviera

Right before midnight on Tuesday, August 11, 1992, a disreputable-looking man parked himself on one of the many folding chairs outside Wilhite's Motel in Panama City, Florida. It's not unusual for tourists to watch the sights along the Redneck Riviera, as this area is sometimes called. But this man was watching with rapt interest the people who passed by on this "Miracle Strip."

After a while the police became interested in watching *him*. They knew this man, and knew that sinister things had happened to more than one woman when he was around. There were whispers of a girl who had disappeared after being seen with him and who was later found murdered.

There was also the story about a local girl who had been talking on a pay phone when he sneaked over and hit her on the head with a hammer. Supposedly he then spirited her off into the woods, and when she regained consciousness, he was raping her. Somehow she talked him into letting her go. The police arrested him, but the young woman had made a couple of minor mistakes when she first described him and the police had to release him.

That's why the Panama City police weren't happy to see him in their area again. They told him to get up and move on, which he did. At least for a while. No one knows for certain whether he came back early the next morning, and whether what then happened at the motel had anything to do with him.

That same evening, even before the man in question sat down outside Wilhite's, a thirty-six-year-old woman named Pamela June Ray was getting ready to leave Villa Rica, Georgia, with her children for a few days' vacation. She was planning to drive overnight to Panama City and stay at a motel.

Pamela Ray had almost canceled the trip after learning her husband, Michael, wasn't going to be able to get time off for a vacation until after September. But she was a devoted mother, and she wanted her two children to spend some time at the beach before they had to return to school. At the last minute she decided to go with her thirty-two-year-old sister, Rhonda, but since Rhonda couldn't leave until Thursday, Pam decided to make the nighttime drive with the children so they could have that extra day at the beach.

Pam's father, Ralph Bennett, a fifty-nine-year-old truck driver, says, "Pam called a motel and said she was fixing to be on the way, and they said they had

REWARD!

Pamela June Ray
Photo courtesy of Helen Bennett

rooms. When Pam got there around five o'clock in the morning, she temporarily locked her two children in her '92 blue Sundance so they'd be safe while she went to make sure she had her room."

As she walked toward Wilhite's Motel, a clerk at White's, the motel next door, saw the 128-pound, five-foot three-inch-tall woman with long brown hair and dark brown eyes, wearing a red tank top, black shorts, and flip-flops. According to her father, Pam was also wearing a diamond necklace, a diamond earring, a diamond wedding ring, a watch with diamonds around the face and on either side, and a three-tier ring embedded with diamonds with a single diamond in the center. The clerk then noticed a man with Pam, and a few minutes later some of the guests at the two motels heard screaming.

"Unsolved Mysteries," the TV series that has successfully ferreted out a number of heinous criminals, covered this case, and while they didn't mention the suspicious man sitting outside Wilhite's, they did uncover another witness to this crime. Their re-creation included a police officer who said he passed the motel around five o'clock that morning and saw Pam standing next to her vehicle talking to a white male.

The officer described the man as being of medium build, with a gray and white striped shirt, sandy hair, and the look of a beach bum. The policeman noticed that the man turned and walked back into the parking lot area of Wilhite's; he saw Pam lock the door with a set of keys in her hand. Then she turned and followed the man into the parking lot.

Five minutes after the policeman left, several guests at Wilhite's were awakened by screams for help, but since the rooms had no phones, no one reported the screams. Only at 8:00 A.M. when Pamela's children were discovered locked in the car outside the motel were the authorities called. By that time the morning rain had washed away any blood, footprints, or other physical evidence that might have told them what had happened a few hours earlier to Pamela June Ray.

Pam's father feels he's getting conflicting and incomplete information from those who might know what

REWARD!

happened that night, especially concerning the man seated on the chair outside Wilhite's. "They're telling so many different tales down there that nobody really knows what happened," he says. All he knows is that he wants his daughter back.

REWARD: $10,000
FROM: Ralph Bennett
FOR: The safe return of Pamela June Ray
CONTACT: Sergeant R. M. Peak
Panama City Beach Police Department
Telephone: (904) 872-3100

The above information is subject to the warning at the beginning of this book.

REWARD
$350,000

26

Find Tiffany, Inc.

At any time in the state of Florida about four thousand youths are listed as missing. In February 1989, when twenty-year-old Tiffany L. Sessions went out for her nightly fast-walk, she became one of them. At 6:00 P.M., wearing a Rolex watch and a white striped sweatshirt saying "Aspen" on it, she left the Casablanca East Apartments in Gainesville, a building in which many University of Florida students lived. She told her roommate she'd return in an hour.

The place where she disappeared "wasn't a little dirt road," says Major Jim Eckert, head of detectives of the Alachua County Sheriff's Office. It was "a well-traveled four-lane highway within a mile or so of Interstate 75 and a major exit ramp from that interstate. Any opportunist could have spotted her and got her into the car."

Tiffany often walked at dusk. The five-foot three-inch, 125-pound girl with shoulder-length blond hair and brown eyes was unconcerned about walking around alone. Just a few years ago, "Gainesville was a relatively peaceful college town," Major Eckert says. "People even left their doors unlocked."

But Gainesville may not have been as quiet as it looked. A year before Tiffany Sessions disappeared, Ted Bundy had considered Gainesville when he was looking for a university town. And a year after Tiffany vanished, a serial killer struck Gainesville and acted so quickly—killing five college students in forty-eight hours—and so brutally, that most newspapers wouldn't even print the details of his grisly crimes.

However, *Vanity Fair* did, saying the Gainesville killer had decapitated one of his victims and "it was rumored that her head had been spiked on the turntable of her stereo with a note in the mouth challenging the police to 'catch me if you can.' Her breasts had been removed, too, and placed on her shelves as bookends, it's said."

What drew these two fiends to Gainesville? Was it really the "relatively peaceful college town" that Eckert claims? Until recently crimes committed on the university campus were covered up. Gainesville had a reputation for heavy drinking and heavy partying, two circumstances virtually guaranteeing student crime, especially of a sexual nature.

In addition, *Vanity Fair* pointed out, "In six surrounding counties to Gainesville are a majority of Florida's state prisons, and a major superhighway . . . is near where Tiffany was jogging." And Florida tends

REWARD!

Tiffany Sessions
Photo courtesy of Alachua County, Florida, Sheriff's Office

to release its prisoners very rapidly, even the most violent ones, because of severe overcrowding.

Eckert stresses that "there's no link at all" between the Sessions case and the Gainesville college killings. He believes that what they're looking for in the Tiffany Sessions case "is a phantom. Typically, if you have a whodunit, you can rely on physical evidence, but we don't have that. You always work a missing persons case as though it were a murder; it may end up that way."

Tiffany's father, a hard-driving businessman, decided to use his marketing skills in an all-out effort to locate his daughter. He and Tiffany had always had a special closeness. Tiffany's parents were divorced when she was one year old, and she became a "military brat" because her mother was in the United States Air Force. Tiffany moved around the country, and she was happy to visit her devoted dad, who even built an apartment in Coconut Grove for Tiffany, next to his house on the waterfront.

When Patrick Sessions realized he might never see his daughter again, he formed a company called Find Tiffany, Inc., to search for her. He enlisted the help of his employer, borrowed a private jet from the chairman of Blockbuster Video, and sought the help of the navy, the marines, the Florida National Guard, the FBI, private investigators, three German shepherds and a bloodhound from the Alachua County Sheriff's Department, and even a psychic.

A $250,000 reward was posted. Voluntary aid came from students, clubs, fraternities, and sororities at the University of Florida, billboard firms, a major public relations firm, businesses such as Alamo-Rent-A-Car and Eckerd Drugstores, and trade organizations such as the National Hotel and Motel Association.

Sessions also set up a toll-free hotline at a cost of $400 a month. He arranged for television public service announcements and distributed a booklet on how to search for missing people. In addition, he recruited celebrities like Miami Dolphins quarterback Dan Marino, Florida Governor Bob Martinez, and television personality John Walsh of "America's Most Wanted" to make personal appeals on behalf of Tiffany.

Nothing worked. As Patrick Sessions says, "Perhaps two thousand of the leads were people saying they saw somebody who looked like Tiffany or who was dressed like Tiffany. Nothing could ever be proved or disproved."

In the five years since that fateful February evening, the world of Patrick and his son, Jason, has been radically changed. "For the first year or so the search for Tiffany was all-consuming. Because the case hasn't been resolved, it is something that eats at you constantly."

In a book he's going to have published, Sessions reminds parents, "You can't put your kid in a bubble. Try to educate your kid to have enough sense. If they're going jogging, they should take along a buddy. Up there where Tiffany was jogging, the next night there were other girls jogging by themselves."

REWARD: $250,000
FROM: Patrick Sessions
FOR: Information leading to the safe return of Tiffany Sessions

REWARD: $100,000
FROM: Patrick Sessions
FOR: Information leading to the arrest and conviction of the person or persons responsible for the kidnapping of Tiffany Sessions
CONTACT: Alachua County Sheriff
              Gainesville, Florida
              Telephone: (904) 336-2500

The above information is subject to the warning at the beginning of this book.

27

Married Against the Mob

Scene: Summer dawn on a residential street in the Long Island, New York, town of East Northport. Several garbage trucks pull out of their places to make their rounds.

Camera tracks to the offices of an independent carting firm. Donald Barstow enters the front door. Gunshots ring out. He falls, shot down in the hallway. More gunshots, these hitting his relative, Robert Kubecka. The gunman disappears.

Kubecka, barely alive, presses a button on a telephone. A policeman answers. Kubecka struggles to whisper into the phone, "I've been shot. Two people have been shot. Send help!" He passes out and collapses on the floor.

Newspaper headlines: "Two Who Fought the Mob Are Murdered!" "Trash Hauler and Relative Killed on

REWARD!

Long Island! Both Aided Investigators Checking Mob Activities!"

This may sound like the opening of a 1930s Warner Brothers gangster movie, but it's a reality. Even the headlines were real. But unlike tidy movies with a sunny ending, so far this doesn't have one because the slayer of Robert Kubecka and his brother-in-law and best friend, Donald Barstow, may still be at large.

In addition, this is not a tale in which the little guy who fights the big mob bosses wins. That may happen only in the movies. This is a story in which corruption won and courage turned out to be foolhardy for those who displayed it. Even if the police do catch the perpetrators—and they feel they're very close to bringing in an indictment—both victims are dead. Too late did these two learn that maverick carting—thumbing their nose at the mob—was a dangerous business.

Robert's father, Jerry Kubecka, had moved to the Huntington area in the early 1950s. At first he worked a dairy route, and then, to earn extra cash, he began hauling his customers' garbage away. However, milk and trash don't mix, and eventually he decided there was more profit in hauling refuse. So he started his own company.

His son, Robert, who had a master's degree in electrical engineering, took over the carting business when his father developed a heart condition. And, according to *Newsday,* a Long Island newspaper, Robert inherited his father's problems with organized crime.

Robert's sister Kathy married Donald Barstow, a budding marine surveyor. Donald quickly took a liking to his new brother-in-law, Robert, and when Donald's surveying work did not take off, he joined the carting company.

"This family business was so convoluted that we were excluded from it," says Belle Barstow, Donald's mother. "Because they were so frightened of what might happen, no one was allowed into the inner circle. We felt the estrangement because our son was pulled away from our family. He had to have new loyalties. It was for protective purposes."

The protection obviously didn't work. Belle Barstow says, "I didn't believe it was going to be as terrible as it turned out to be." At the joint funerals, Robert's ailing father, Jerry, stressed that "I cannot, I will not, testify," referring to the murder investigation. "I have to keep strong for my family. I have fought them [presumably the mob] for many years. Maybe I overdid it. But I will not testify now," he was quoted as saying.

Robert Kubecka had always been a rebel hauler. His fight was a continuing battle with a trade group called the Private Sanitation Industry of Nassau-Suffolk. Federal, state, and local investigations into those individuals and organizations have gone on for years.

Part of the government's secret ammunition may have been Barstow and Kubecka. Deborah Lee, a neighbor of Barstow's parents who helped set up a reward fund for information about their killer, says, "These two men refused to play ball. They were wearing wires [body microphones], actively involving themselves in investigations against the Mafia, testifying against them. Somebody put them out of their activity."

The victims probably knew who their killers were.

REWARD!

On August 9, 1989, the evening before the murders, Robert Kubecka received a threatening phone call. After the shooting, the *New York Times* stated that the mortally wounded Kubecka offered a brief description of the assailant to the police on the phone. At the scene police also found a small bag and a trace of blood that belonged to neither of the victims.

Police expect to soon close in on Salvatore "The Golfer" Avellino, age fifty-seven, of St. James, Long Island, but even if they do, they still need more information. Avellino is described by police as a captain in the Lucchese crime family, and in some quarters he is deemed to be the active boss of the carting industry in Nassau and Suffolk counties.

The reward fund is now about $20,000, and information can be submitted anonymously. Detective Norman Rein of the Suffolk County Police Department says, "A third-party attorney could administer the information."

Police started to move in on Avellino during the winter of 1993. His assets were seized, and he was enjoined from participating any further in the carting business. Says Detective Rein, Avellino "was one of the few people convicted as a result of the Kubecka and Barstow testimony back in the mid-1980s," and for that Avellino did community service.

Friends of Kubecka and Barstow said that both of the men were looking to get out of the carting business, that the pressures and the commitment weren't worth it. "They weren't out to be rich," the friends say. "They weren't out to be powerful."

REWARD!

REWARD: Approximately $20,000
FROM: A fund set up by friends and neighbors
FOR: Indictment and conviction of the killers of Donald Bar-
stow and Robert Kubecka
CONTACT: Suffolk County Police Homicide Squad
Telephone: (516) 852-6395

The above information is subject to the warning at the beginning
of this book.

REWARD
Up to $1,000

28

Mysteries
for a Mother

A couple of weeks before she died, her behavior seemed to change radically," says Marlene Przybylak (pronounced Priz-black), a secretary for the state of California and the mother of nine-year-old Amanda Leigh Gaeke. "She started having temper tantrums and trouble paying attention in school, along with nightmares that someone was taking her away.

"But now I wonder whether someone she knew, maybe at school, was molesting her," she says of her daughter, who had light green eyes and blond hair, which she wore in a ponytail. "I read that when [children are] molested, their behavior often changes."

Marlene Przybylak would never find out the answer to her speculations. On October 3, 1991, her daughter didn't return to her home at 3130 Landis Street in San Diego, California. So around 7:30 P.M., Marlene went

REWARD!

Amanda Leigh Gaeke
Photo courtesy of Marlene Przybylak-Price

out frantically looking for Mandy. That was when the first of several unexplained events occurred. "My mother called our house then," Marlene says. "And she swears Mandy picked up the phone and said, 'Mommy's going to be home soon.' And then my mother says she heard doors slam as if more than one person had come into our house. And Mandy told her, 'I think that's Mom coming now,' and she hung up."

To complicate the mystery, other children in school later reported that they had seen Mandy get into a red truck after school. If true, this means she probably never went home at all. "I didn't know what to believe," says Mrs. Przybylak. In addition, "the psychics came out of the woodwork, leading the family on wild-goose chases. They were all saying she was alive and telling us where we would find her, but we didn't.

"For days I was a walking zombie," Marlene Przybylak says. She had to hide her mounting hysteria so as not to upset her other daughter, especially on her birthday. "We tried to go on with her planned party, but everyone had tears in their eyes."

She also had to face the distressing job of going through Mandy's clothes to figure out what she was wearing when she disappeared. "I had to look through everything she owned and figure out what was missing. I cried going through each piece of clothing."

What she had most feared happened eleven days after Mandy vanished. "Some officers who were with me said, 'We want you to sit down. We found a body.' I said, 'Is it a man, a woman, or a child?' They said, 'We can't tell . . . yet.' I waited until six, and when I saw the coroner come to our door in a suit, I knew."

Mandy had been murdered by asphyxiation. Her body was found nude with evidence of sexual molestation. Another mystery for the mother is why she wasn't found sooner. "She was found less than six blocks from our house in a yard surrounded by houses. The police think she was murdered the night she disappeared or the next morning, so she was there the whole time. I don't know how the people who lived nearby could have missed it," she says, shaking her head in disbelief.

One small bit of consolation for the mother was that "there's a fence around the area where she was found, and strangers started putting crosses and flowers on it. Children left her handmade cards, saying things like 'I miss you' and 'You'll be safe in heaven.' Others wrote notes to the killer saying things like 'You don't deserve to live on this earth.'"

Many unanswered questions still bother Mrs. Przybylak. "Was Mandy taken from our house or did she go into someone's truck earlier? I believe she wouldn't have gone with a stranger. If somebody tried to make Mandy do what she didn't want, she would scream or run like hell. But maybe she knew the person she went off with," she speculates.

Mrs. Przybylak despairs of ever solving all these puzzles. Or finding the killer. "When a case like this goes unsolved, new cases come up, and the police don't have time for your child's case," she says with a sigh. "The public wants to forget it, and they put it on the back burner of their minds hoping it will fade away. But it doesn't fade away in *my* mind."

Then she lowers her voice and pleads, "If only we could find out who did it, I could put that part to rest and try to get on, instead of wondering all the time who out there did it and why are they out free while my Mandy is six feet under the ground."

REWARD: Up to $1,000
FROM: San Diego Crime Stoppers
FOR: Information leading to the arrest or conviction of the killer of Amanda Leigh Gaeke
CONTACT: San Diego Crime Stoppers
Telephone: (619) 235-TIPS

The above information is subject to the warning at the beginning of this book.

REWARD
$11,000

29

Stubbed Out in Portland

On the January evening in 1990 when blues legend John Lee Hooker was the sold-out attraction at a nightclub in Portland, Oregon, called Starry Night, 180 fake tickets were presented at the door. Three days later an employee of that music club, Tim Moreau, vanished and has not been seen since. The big question in Portland is whether or not there was a connection between the two events.

Tim Moreau, a tall, good-looking, redheaded former Eagle Scout, was twenty-one when he disappeared. Although he was near the top of his class at Reed College in Portland, his father, Mike Moreau, says, "He decided in his junior year to take a two-year leave of absence from college to work full-time in the local music business."

REWARD!

In February 1990 Moreau's car was discovered at Portland International Airport. Moreau's disappearance and his possible connection with the counterfeit ticket scam have provided the elements of a mystery that has kept the music and dance scene in Portland hopping for three years.

"Tim was very straightforward," says his father, Mike. "We think there may be a possibility that he got sucked into counterfeiting tickets." But even if he did commit the crime, his father ponders whether his son would truly have gone to such lengths as to totally disappear because of a minor counterfeiting incident. The criminal charges for what Tim did—if indeed he did it—would only have been a Class C felony, which was unlikely to result in prison time for a first offender.

Portland Police Detective Steve Baumgarte admits, "With the evidence we had, we would not have been successful in prosecuting anyone for the ticket scheme without Moreau's assistance. No Moreau, no prosecutable case." And now the statute of limitations has expired on the fraud issue. "If Moreau were to walk in here today, there would be no prosecutable case for fraud" against him or anyone else.

But no one expects to ever see Tim Moreau again. Most think his disappearance is permanent. After all, if Tim Moreau had been planning to flee and start up somewhere else, people wonder why he would have left all his personal items, including credit cards and checkbook, behind in his apartment.

Adding to the mysteries, another former Starry Night employee told police they would find Tim's body at the bottom of the river weighted down by micro-

REWARD!

Tim Moreau
Photo by Greg Random Studio, New Orleans,
Louisiana, courtesy of Charles and Penny Moreau

phone stands. When the river was dragged, there were more headlines but nothing was found.

These are some of the plausible reasons for Tim Moreau's disappearance:

1. *Suicide.* Tim Moreau's family, friends, and associates agree that Tim wasn't likely to kill himself. And how he would have disposed of his own body is a puzzle.

2. *Flight.* With his Eagle Scout training, he could be in hiding, surviving by his wits. But since the penalties for his crime weren't great before, and are non-

existent now, there appears to be no need for him to have disappeared.

3. *Murder.* There could be a darker reason for Tim's disappearance, which would have led someone to kill him. But there is no body and no evidence of murder.

"We can't imagine that one person murdered him," says his mother. "He's over six feet tall. You'd have to have help disposing of the body." His father speculates that there are at least two people out there who know what happened to Tim.

"We're optimistic that someday we'll know what happened. We'll do whatever we can to keep the story alive," say his parents, social service professionals living in Louisiana. But Mike Moreau adds dispiritedly, "We've resigned ourselves to the fact that Tim is dead. For a period of time we really wanted to believe that perhaps he was still alive. But there's just too much evidence that would lead us finally to conclude that we'll never see him again."

REWARD: $11,000
FROM: Mike and Penny Moreau, $10,000; The Portland Police Department's Crime Stoppers Program, $1,000
FOR: Information leading to the conviction of the person or persons who killed Tim Moreau
CONTACT: Crime Stoppers
Telephone: (503) 823-HELP

The above information is subject to the warning at the beginning of this book.

REWARD
$4,000–$10,000
(Canadian dollars)
Portion of $240,000
(Canadian dollars)

30

Hell on the Highways

Since Canada is so much safer than the United States, one would think Canadians would be in less danger on their highways. Although that's probably true in general, it wasn't so for three women, one of whom seems to have been abducted and burned by two men who happened by, a second who was most likely murdered while hitchhiking, and a third who was struck by a hit-and-run truck driver.

Lynda Shaw

Ontario student Lynda Shaw, age twenty-one, was abducted during Easter weekend while on her way back to school after spending a holiday break with her family. She was scheduled to take an exam the following morning, April 16, 1990, at the University of Western Ontario; instead, her burned body was found in a farmer's field days later.

Until Lynda Shaw's murder, drivers felt perfectly safe traveling on Highway 401 at any time of the day or night. So Lynda probably wasn't worried when she left her home in Huttonville at 11:15 at night and headed west on Highway 401 toward London, Ontario. The car trip generally takes an hour and a half or so.

According to the Toronto *Sun,* eight minutes after leaving home she stopped for gas in Milton. An hour later she left a Burger King restaurant in a service area on the highway. While she was there, police believe someone let the air out of her right front tire. A few minutes after she returned to the highway, she pulled over onto the shoulder of the road because of the soft tire, but she continued driving, looking for a place to change her tire.

At about 12:35 A.M., she stopped near the Middlesex-Oxford county line and began to change the tire. Many passing motorists later told police they saw Lynda on her knees beside the front tire, a man standing at the front of the car, and a dark pickup truck parked near it.

An hour later witnesses reported seeing another car, a gold 1974 Chrysler Newport, near Shaw as she tried to fix her flat. An hour after that, a truck driver saw this same Chrysler drive away from Shaw's car and pull off 401 onto Dorchester Road. Others also saw this car in the area early that morning.

At about 6:30 A.M., a woman resembling Lynda Shaw was seen walking in a ditch across the highway

REWARD!

Lynda Shaw
Photo from Canada Wide Feature Services Limited

from her car. She appeared to be frightened. A half hour later a motorist saw a thin wisp of smoke rising in the air near the dead-end road. Police believe it was Lynda Shaw's body being set on fire.

Almost a full day later, at 4:00 A.M., witnesses saw a dark-colored car and a truck near the same dead-end road, at the site of what appeared to be a large fireball. Police believe that Lynda's body had been burned a second time. A witness also saw two men at the location of the fire, one walking away.

Lynda's burned body was later found by a farmer. She had died of multiple injuries, including stab wounds. According to Constable Ray Dobbs of the Ontario Provincial Police, "She was burned to eliminate evidence and hinder police identification of the victim." Nonetheless, she was identified through dental records.

A dark blue duffel coat, size 42, was found near the burned body. Detectives said it was one of about 1,250 coats sold by Sears in the late 1970s and could not be traced because the store didn't save old sales records.

Two years after the murder, a letter signed by a Jim Gold, who claimed to be the killer, came to the attention of the police. The letter contained information that only the killer or someone close to him would know. Jim Gold has never been found.

Based on descriptions—especially from the man who sold that used Chrysler Newport—one of the suspects is six feet two inches tall, weighs 180 to 190 pounds, is in his late thirties, and has deep-set dark brown eyes, high cheekbones, a prominent jaw, a thick lower lip, and yellowed teeth, possibly from nicotine. Ontario Provincial Police say he wasn't clean-shaven and wore a green baseball cap with a white crest.

Lynda's mother, Carol Taylor, made a passionate videotaped appeal for her daughter's killer to come forward. "I believe you have suffered in the past and are suffering now," she said to the murderer. "I fear that if you don't get the help you need soon, you may do something like this again."

REWARD!

Cindy Halliday

Lynda Shaw was slain on Easter weekend in Ontario. Two years later, on Easter Monday 1992, seventeen-year-old Cindy Halliday vanished. She was on her way, probably hitchhiking, along Highway 27 from Barrie to her mother's home, twenty miles north, in Waverley. Police believe her body was dumped in a reforestation area in Vespra Township, where it was eaten by animals.

What was left of her and her belongings was found piecemeal. A month after her disappearance, a man came upon her wallet. Her jacket was recovered two weeks later, and a month after that, a man walking his dog was stunned by the gruesome discovery of her skull. Other bone fragments, hair, and clothing were located soon afterward, among straight rows of pine trees.

Cindy, who had a history as a teenage runaway, had a tough side to her nature that made her fearless enough to hitchhike. According to the Toronto *Star,* she had gone to Barrie to visit her boyfriend who was in prison on an assault charge, before hitchhiking north to Waverley, to a home she would never reach.

At first her death was ignored by the media, probably because of her "tough girl" image. But then a small local newspaper, the Barrie *Advance,* printed a story about her. Readers learned that Toronto-born Cindy was obsessed with Canada's favorite sport, hockey. After wearing a hockey uniform for the first time at the age of six and a half, she became such a good player that at times she was even sought out as goalie for a boys' team.

REWARD!

In school, however, she did not fare so well. She was assigned to special classes because of her reading difficulties and her boisterous conduct. "She was the type of person you knew was around," her mother, Jackie, says proudly. "Always talking with her gravelly voice, always on the go. She couldn't sit still very long," she admitted. "On the outside she put on a tough act, but if you really knew her, you realized it was just a front. Actually she liked to hug and wasn't afraid to say 'I love you.'"

But, as her friends told Lori Martin of the Barrie *Advance,* just because Cindy seemed tough, "it doesn't mean she deserved to die."

Cindy Halliday
Photo courtesy of Jackie Halliday Hinds

REWARD!

After the chain of newspapers for which Lori Martin works posted a reward to help find the killer, there was a flood of leads, and twenty-eight sightings of her hitchhiking that night were reported to the Ontario Provincial Police. Three witnesses reported seeing her in a light-colored Chrysler LeBaron or Dodge Diplomat, possibly a 1979 to 1981 model.

A speculative portrait of her abductor-killer was also drawn up: a male in his mid-twenties to early thirties, someone possibly known to Cindy. And he may be familiar with the forest in which her remains were found.

Cindy was last seen wearing a red, white, and blue jacket, red sweatpants, a white turtleneck under a red sweatshirt, brown deck shoes, and white socks. She was five feet nine and weighed about 130 pounds. She had blue eyes and shoulder-length brown hair.

Because the killing occurred on Easter weekend, the question naturally arose whether one individual might be responsible for killing Lynda Shaw in 1990 and Cindy Halliday in 1992. But Constable Bill Crozier says, "So far we haven't been able to link our case with the other."

Pierina Argentini

For Giorgio Argentini, the Christmas season is a tragic time. He is slowly recovering from the Sunday, December 23, 1991, hit-and-run death of his dark-haired wife, Pierina. Three months passed before he could open her Christmas gifts, and five months before he could sleep in their bed again.

REWARD!

Pierina Argentini
Photo from Canada Wide Feature
Services Limited

Two nights before Christmas Eve, he and Pierina were getting ready for bed at eleven o'clock when she realized they'd left the baby's bottle and diaper liners at a family gathering. "I offered to go out," says Giorgio, "but she wanted face-cream remover and she decided to see what was on sale at the pharmacy. So we kissed and I told her 'Take care.'"

Somewhere between their condo in Etobicoke, a suburb of Toronto, and an all-night drugstore a fifteen-minute drive away, twenty-three-year-old Pierina, a legal secretary, apparently stopped her beige 1992 Nissan van on Highway 27. It's believed she was looking for help in changing a flat tire.

REWARD!

When Giorgio awoke at 5:20 A.M., he realized Pierina hadn't returned. He searched the streets, the drugstore, everywhere, before dawn. "I thought the worst—that she'd been abducted," he told the Toronto *Star*.

In midmorning, a taxi driver found Pierina's body on the shoulder of Highway 27, three-quarters of a mile from her van. She had bled to death. She was killed, say police, by "a large commercial truck with distinctive markings and features," including a customized pattern of reflectors, perhaps purchased in a truck accessory shop.

Constable Yule of the Ontario Provincial Police says he is sure that the driver must have known he'd hit something but that he didn't stop to investigate. The truck probably knocked Pierina unconscious. Perhaps it even threw her body or dragged it along the highway, and she may have lain on the shoulder of the road for as many as four hours before expiring.

Since this highway is a major route across the border to the United States, American vehicles have also been under surveillance. Perhaps Monsignor John Iverinci was referring to Americans during the funeral service for Pierina when he said, "How unchristian are the pirates of the road. . . . A simple gesture of compassion would have saved her life."

"When things like this happen," reflects Giorgio, "you kinda wonder. Is there someone up there looking after us? Pierina never did anything wrong in her life." Andrew, the son whose needs she had gone out to attend, "knows where his mother is now—at the cemetery. 'We're going to see Mommy,' he says when we

REWARD!

go for a visit. He kisses the gravestone and her picture there."

Giorgio says, "One year after the accident, Andrew became emotional for the first time. He was crying and touching the gravestone and whispering to his mother, 'Come home with us.'"

REWARD: $10,000 (Canadian dollars)
FROM: Metroland Printing, Publishing and Distributing
FOR: Information leading to the arrest and conviction of the killer or killers of Cindy Halliday
CONTACT: Elmvale, Ontario, Provincial Police
            Telephone: (705) 322-2424

REWARD: A portion of a $240,000 reward fund (Canadian dollars)
FROM: The St. Mary's Rotary Club
FOR: Rewards for information in the slayings of two other women are now being offered to seek clues in the 1990 murder of Lynda Shaw
CONTACT: Constable Ray Dobbs, Ontario Provincial Police
            Telephone: (519) 539-9811

REWARD: $4,000 (Canadian dollars)
FROM: The Ontario Provincial Police, $2,500; and Crime Stoppers, $1,500
FOR: Information leading to the arrest and conviction of the hit-and-run driver who killed Pierina Argentini
CONTACT: Ontario Provincial Police
            Telephone: (416) 278-6131
            or Crime Stoppers
            Telephone: (416) 222-8477

The above information is subject to the warning at the beginning of this book.

REWARD
$11,000

31

Nicky No-Socks

Here's a guy who goes to the market to get some fruit for his nine kids, and there are two people arguing and he wants to be the peacemaker. So he gets shot and killed for trying to be a good guy and break up the fight," says Detective Dennis Mulloy of New York City's 69th Police Precinct.

Abdul Mateen was the pacifier-turned-victim at Brooklyn's Terminal Market on May 25, 1990, at about 5:00 P.M. According to witnesses Mateen was shot by forty-six-year-old Nicholas Facciolo of Farragut Road, Brooklyn. Facciolo fled and has not been apprehended. A year later Facciolo's brother, Bruno, known to be connected with organized crime, was himself a victim of homicide, found stuffed in a car trunk.

In February 1993, three years after Mateen's slaying, Detective Mulloy says that the police are still ac-

REWARD!

Nicholas Facciolo
Photo from files of New York Police Department,
provided by Charles Rogers, the Canarsie *Courier*

tively looking for Nicholas Facciolo. "As of late, everyone's saying he's possibly around. We've made several attempts to grab him. We haven't been fortunate enough to arrest him."

The alleged killer's nickname describes him best: Nicky No-Socks. According to Charles Rogers, staff writer of a neighborhood newspaper, the Canarsie *Courier*, "He always walked around without socks on, and wore sneakers or tennis shoes." He is of medium build, five feet ten, 150 pounds, with dark salt-and-

REWARD!

pepper hair. His brown eyes are usually hidden behind sunglasses.

The mayor's office offered a $10,000 reward and the Police Department's Crimestoppers Office will pay $1,000 for information leading to the arrest and indictment of the suspect. Because of the potential link to organized crime, informants can withhold their names and will be paid by a code number.

REWARD: $11,000
FROM: The Office of the Mayor of the City of New York, $10,000; City Police Department's Crimestoppers Office, $1,000
FOR: Information leading to the arrest and indictment of Nicholas Facciolo
CONTACT: 24-Hour Hot Line: (718) 287-0311
Crimestoppers: (212) 577-TIPS
69th Precinct: (718) 257-6215

The above information is subject to the warning at the beginning of this book.

REWARD
$100,000 (Canadian dollars)

32

The Deadly Drifter

The mention of Dennis Melvyn Howe's name evokes almost as much recognition in Canada as Charles Manson's does in the United States, even though Howe is suspected of having committed only one murder. So far.

His infamy started with the stunning discovery of the decomposing body of nine-year-old Sharin' Morningstar Keenan, stuffed in a rooming-house refrigerator. The weird drifter who rented the room is still on the loose over ten years after that dreadful day.

Dennis Melvyn Howe is also known as Michael Burns, Wayne King, Ralph Ferguson, and Jim Meyers; he has a host of other aliases as well. Some investigators think he may now be in the United States, possibly in Florida or some other southern state. Because

REWARD!

Toronto police say Howe is one of the slickest cover-up artists they've ever encountered, it is possible that Howe has been involved in a number of crimes in the United States that have not yet been pinned on him.

Sharin', his only known victim, was the oldest of three children of Brendan Caron and Lynda Keenan. The other children of this common-law couple of former hippies are a girl named Celeste and a boy called Summer Sky.

Sharin', a fourth grader, disappeared on January 23, 1983, after her mother left her at about three o'clock in Jean Sibelius park, a playground near her home in the Casa Loma district of Toronto. An hour later, when her father walked over to the park to bring her home, he found the playground empty.

Since Sharin' always told her folks where she was going, her father informed the police immediately. By 6:15 a full-fledged search for Sharin' was started. Fears of abduction by a pedophile were raised when a witness nearby told police that he'd seen a girl, answering Sharin's description, talking with an adult male who seemed to be coaxing her to go with him.

Nine days after Sharin' disappeared, tenants in a rooming house told one team of investigators that "Michael Burns" hadn't been seen since January 24, the day after Sharin' disappeared. When the police went in to examine the premises, they found Sharin's body in the refrigerator, wrapped in a green plastic garbage bag. She had been raped and strangled.

"Never, never will I ever forget seeing that body in that fridge," Staff Sergeant Wayne Oldham told the Toronto *Star*. "It left such an indelible impression on

REWARD!

Dennis Melvyn Howe
Canada Wide Feature Services Limited

my whole being. I am going to be relentless" in the pursuit of the murderer, he promised.

After a month of extraordinary detective work, the police learned the true identity of the man in the rooming house on Brunswick Avenue. He was Dennis Melvyn Howe. His father, Wilfrid Clifford Howe, had been a sex offender who, according to the Toronto *Sun,* had been sent to prison for having sex with Dennis's half sister.

Dennis Howe's criminal career started when he was a teenager with convictions for break-ins, robberies, rape, and abduction. He had spent half of his adult years in prison, and had disappeared in Saskatchewan, where he was born, after he was paroled from prison, with deadly results. Strangely, in the ten years since he left that rooming house, he has never been seen again, despite a $100,000 reward and one of the most far-reaching public campaigns in Canadian history.

That Howe has remained a fugitive for so long is surprising, because he shouldn't be difficult to find, even though his description is a decade old. His puffy face was plastered all over Canada's bus shelters and on American TV. His fingerprints were dispatched all over the world. And a lot is known about him.

He is five feet nine inches tall, weighs about 165 pounds, and has a tanned, leathery complexion and brown eyes. His thinning brown hair is graying at the sides. He wears it stylishly long or in a brush cut. He has a wrinkled forehead, a small gap between his front teeth, a partial upper denture, a hairy chest and arms, squared shoulders, and a cleft chin with a scar on it. He is left-handed, known to wear a mustache, and has crooked little fingers.

He drank Molson's beer and chain-smoked Player's plain cigarettes. He was a loudmouth who called everyone and everything a "turkey"; at other times he transformed himself into a withdrawn loner. He's known as a "supreme con man and quick-change artist" who's good at concocting stories and covering his tracks.

Howe is now fifty-three years old. When not in prison, he has worked as a stock clerk, cook, roofer, janitor, millwright, electrician, carpenter, and metal worker.

If you run into someone who fits this description, call David Boothby of the Metropolitan Toronto Police

REWARD!

right away. He's been waiting for your call for ten years.

REWARD: $100,000 (Canadian dollars)
FROM: Metropolitan Toronto Police
FOR: The arrest and conviction of Dennis Melvyn Howe
CONTACT: David Boothby, Metropolitan Toronto Police
Telephone: (416) 324-6218

The above information is subject to the warning at the beginning of this book.

REWARD
$10,000

33

The Pusher's Sister

This is an old case, but it's an interesting one and there are still plenty of clues. "On December 23, 1981, a woman by the name of Roxann Jeeves left her apartment in Dallas, Texas, with her six-year-old son, Kristopher," says Lieutenant Larry Forsyth, who has been obsessed with this case for more than a decade.

"Roxann was a thirty-year-old divorced insurance underwriter who was planning to remarry. She was taking her son to meet his new grandmother in Kansas." A witness saw Kristopher leave the house, and at the same time she "noticed a black male walking with a Mexican or Indian female who had a black eye. They looked like street people and didn't fit in."

The witness looked back and saw that the man was now holding Kristopher's hand, and the three were all walking toward the back of the building, toward

REWARD!

Sketch of suspected killer of Roxann Jeeves
Sketch courtesy of Lieutenant Larry Forsyth,
Criminal Investigation Division, Dallas, Texas

Roxann's car. Forsyth says, "Roxann walked down to
the car to join her son and found this situation."

Forsyth continues, "A few minutes later, around two
and a half miles away, we have Roxann, who is white,
driving her '78 blue Thunderbird with a tan top into a
gas station. This same black man is with her, the other
woman is gone, and Kristopher is in the back seat.
The attendant remembers that Roxann appeared nervous, but she said nothing. Roxann purchased some
gas and left with the man around eleven A.M.

"At eleven forty-five a patrol office noticed an abandoned Thunderbird. About one hundred feet away, he found the bodies of Roxann and her son, Kristopher, both of whom had been murdered. Roxann had not been robbed or sexually assaulted.

"We later learned that our killer then walked six miles to a Mobil gas station at the corner of Bruton and Highway 635. He made a telephone call from a pay phone, and fifteen or twenty minutes later was picked up by a heavyset black male with long hair and possibly dreadlocks driving a faded green 1954 Buick."

Forsyth says that "subsequent investigation told us that our killer, the man who had come to her apartment, had been in that complex three days before the murder. At that time the killer purchased a bag of marijuana from a neighbor. He also bought more marijuana the morning of the murder."

Enter Roxann's twenty-three-year-old brother, Kurt. "Kurt lived with Roxann for about six months, but she had kicked him out three months before she was murdered, probably because of his drug problems. And Kurt also had some marijuana dealings with some people in Roxann's apartment complex.

"We believe that Kurt may have sold some marijuana for these people and not paid his bill. We also know that Kurt associated only with blacks, and that after Kurt left Roxann's apartment, a black man came to the complex late at night and knocked on Roxann's door looking for Kurt."

Lieutenant Forsyth interviewed Kurt, "but he told me that he had no knowledge of his sister's murder. He jumped up and left the interview." Lieutenant Forsyth

REWARD!

**Sketch of female companion of
suspected killer of Roxann Jeeves**
Sketch provided by Lieutenant Larry Forsyth,
Criminal Investigation Division, Dallas, Texas

backed off on Kurt, and then, he said, "Kurt is convicted of a drug-related charge, goes to prison, gets
out on April 18, 1984, and goes right to a black section
of town. He flashes a roll of cash to buy some marijuana, and within six hours he is murdered. Whatever
information he had went to his grave with him"—along
with Forsyth's best hope of solving this case rapidly.

Still, there are some outstanding clues. The killer
was in his early to middle thirties, had frizzy shoulder-
length hair, probably wore a pinky ring in the shape
of a horseshoe, had a heavy keloid scar down the middle of his right hand, and called himself G-man.

The man who picked up the killer at the gas station drove a four-door 1954 Buick with faded green paint and rear fins. "That kind of car was rare in 1981," Forsyth points out.

The killer also left several items behind that are believed to have been stolen before 1981, and it might help if Forsyth could find out who they were stolen from.

"There was a holster with some markings. These furrows led experts to believe the murder weapon was an antique .38 Smith and Wesson, probably what they call a five-screw. It's not your normal Saturday night special," he adds.

The killer also left a bag behind, and Forsyth is looking for someone who kept formaldehyde in a lemon extract bottle. "Back then it was popular in the lower sections of town to lace a marijuana cigarette with formaldehyde. It was called a Sherman Stick, supposedly because the high was like being hit by a Sherman tank." So this man smoked that.

He also owned a black knit stocking cap with a decorative pin on it saying "Super Shit." Forsyth says, "I know that today we put things on bumper stickers that we wouldn't have ten years ago—like 'Shit happens.' But in 1981, his pin was unusual."

Lieutenant Forsyth paused, then went on: "I do not want to retire without clearing this case. It has haunted me since I got it, because you think about the horror that the mother went through probably watching the child murdered before her eyes. You think about the things the child had going through his mind when he saw the man with the gun. That was his birthday and

REWARD!

he got his brains blown out. All of the emotions that a child of that age is supposed to be experiencing, and he experienced just the opposite, something very horrible. And the person who would commit an offense like this, he and I need to talk real bad."

REWARD: $10,000
FROM: Schepps Dairy
FOR: The arrest and indictment of the killer of Roxann and Kristopher Jeeves
CONTACT: Lieutenant Larry Forsyth
　　　　　　　Criminal Investigation Division
　　　　　　　Dallas, Texas
　　　　　　　Telephone: (214) 653-2745

The above information is subject to the warning at the beginning of this book.

REWARD
$1,000–$28,400

34

The Serial Killers Who Can't Be Stopped

Two famous serial killers of prostitutes—Washington's Green River Killer and the Midwest's I-71 Truck Stop Killer—claimed over fifty victims. Although there are many dissimilarities in the way the two operated, both chose prostitutes as victims, both tortured the women before killing them, and both ignominiously dumped the bodies. Some believe these killers may have been one and the same.

The Green River Killer

It has been estimated that as many as a hundred serial killers could be roaming the United States at any one time. The Green River Killer was certainly one of the most successful, if number of victims and ability to elude capture are the criteria.

REWARD!

In the state of Washington, only decomposing flesh and bones remained of at least forty-nine prostitutes who disappeared in the early 1980s. Many of them were found strangled, bound, and submerged in the Green River, and there was evidence of sexual assault; several had pyramid-shaped rocks placed inside their vaginas.

Now, more than twelve years after the first of these brutal homicides was discovered, the Green River Killer has still not been identified, let alone apprehended. He may still be on the loose, perhaps murdering prostitutes he picks up at truck stops in the Midwest.

Or possibly he's continuing his fiendish spree in Washington State. Although most Washingtonians assume that the killings ended with the original forty-nine slayings, more than two dozen prostitutes have been victims of unsolved murders in the Seattle area in the last two years.

Carol Osrom of the Seattle *Times* profiled the earlier victims of the Green River Killer. They were from low-income homes where alcohol and abuse were common. All of them had been juvenile offenders, charged with underage drinking, drug abuse, shoplifting, or similar petty crimes.

All of the first five prostitutes found dead were connected with the Sea-Tac strip between Seattle-Tacoma International Airport and Pacific Highway South. Most of the remains were found near illegal dumping places. Some of the victims had not even been reported missing, for most had been transients, without permanent addresses.

REWARD!

"In August of 1982 few thought to connect this problem of missing teenagers with the murders, so ordinary and common were the reports of the missing. . . . The failure to make this connection proved to be a major breakdown of the system," wrote Carlton Smith and Tomas Guillen in *The Search for the Green River Killer.*

"If . . . the mayor and four city council members [had died], the story would have remained very hot in the news for a long period of time," says Bryan Johnson, director of KOMO Radio in the mid-1980s. "It wasn't until two or three years after the killings had stopped that there was a feeling there was a full-blown serial killer here," Johnson adds.

And a very disturbed one at that, said FBI serial killer experts, alluding to the stones the killer had inserted in his victims. The FBI profile on the Green River Killer also included the suggestion that he was probably an outdoor type, and possibly also religious; he could have been "baptizing" his early victims by putting them into the Green River after he killed them. And, FBI analysis said, he was most likely in his mid-twenties to early thirties.

It is probable he also felt he had a mission—to cleanse the streets of prostitutes. Women's groups such as COYOTE (Come Off Your Old Tired Ethics), which fight discrimination against prostitutes, have pointed out that the victims' profession obviously caused delays in the investigations. These groups charged that because the women were prostitutes, nobody cared enough about them to find their killers.

Although these allegations were probably right to

some degree, finding a killer of prostitutes is never easy. Prostitutes go off with strangers without telling anyone where they're going. And afterward, since no one knows they're gone, no one searches diligently for them. Furthermore, overburdened law enforcement agents are more likely to focus on "sympathetic victims," especially those cases that the public is screaming to have solved.

Besides, there was nothing to go on except this killer's presumed hatred of hookers and his bizarre actions. That is, there was little concrete information on the Green River Killer until April 1984, when fresh footprints were found, distinctive ones made by a size 10 or 11 composition-sole shoe. But while this caused some excitement, the clue did not prove sufficient to help police catch the killer.

The Green River Killer went right back to what he had been doing, unimpeded. Then, just as investigators despaired of ever finding him, the murders stopped in May 1985, three years after the first killings. But the Green River Killer's victims—women who had been missing since 1982 and 1983—continued to be found in Washington as late as 1986.

But have the killings really stopped? And did they start in the early 1980s—or had they started even earlier? King County's Green River Task Force Captain Frank Adamson believes that the serial murders started well before those credited to the Green River Killer. He believes that thirty-eight unsolved murders committed between 1973 and 1982 could very well be linked.

And in determining whether the Green River Killer

quit, one has to consider the copycat killings that sprang up in Portland, Oregon, where seventeen slayings were reported, along with serial slayings of prostitutes in Vancouver, British Columbia; in San Diego, California; and in the Midwest near Interstate 71, a series of killings described below. All of these murders were supposedly the work of other people. Supposedly.

On the other hand, some people believe the Green River killings actually were the work of more than one serial killer. Bryan Johnson noted that three different groups of women were killed—the five bodies found in the Green River, the four found at Star Lake, and the remaining forty found at dumping sites. He speculates that three or more killers were roaming the state.

Although thousands of names have been cleared, the television newsmagazine "20/20" revealed in 1989 that "of the eighteen thousand names in its files, the task force still has to look at more than six thousand." And as Bryan Johnson mentions, "You really need the manpower to follow them up. They're [the task force] down to one or two people who are now working the case part-time."

When former FBI serial-killer specialist Bob Ressler, who helped author Thomas Harris in his research for *The Silence of the Lambs*, appeared on "Larry King Live" in April 1991, he said, "A person who would just stop doing what he has done over such a long period of time . . . has to be in jail. He'd have to be dead. He'd have to be in a different part of the world. I just don't believe that they would cold-turkey something like that."

REWARD!

Maybe the killer didn't stop committing murder. Bryan Johnson ponders whether "the killings stopped in 1984 or whether the King County Task Force just *says* they had stopped? It is a matter of serious debate around here," he says, pointing to the unsolved murders of twelve prostitutes in Snohomish County and fifteen to twenty in King County in the past two years.

The I-71 Truck Stop Killer

The timing of when the killing of the Washington prostitutes stopped and similar killings began in the Midwest dovetails nicely, although these crimes were a little different. The Truck Stop Killer did seek out prostitutes, but instead of immediately dumping his victims, he sometimes kept their bodies with him for a while. One victim, who was six months pregnant when she was killed, was slain within two days of her disappearance. Yet, according to the medical examiners, her body had been kept refrigerated for nearly a month.

Not only did this killer keep some of the bodies with him, but he also kept their clothes. The same item of clothing was taken from all of the murdered women, although the police will not reveal what it was, hoping this detail will one day help them identify the killer.

As with the Green River Killer, at first no one even realized there was a murderer at large in the Midwest. The killings, which started in 1985, were initially thought to be random. Only in 1990 did Michael Berens, a reporter for the Columbus, Ohio, *Dispatch,* cross-check the deaths and spot the pattern.

REWARD!

"No one can say for certain, but I saw that the evidence was overwhelming that there was just one person," Berens says. "When three prostitutes disappear from the same trailer park and the police are saying it's random, you begin to wonder." He notes that these serial killings would ultimately include dozens of other victims in several states.

One reason it was hard to spot a pattern, at least in Ohio, was that the eight murdered women were scattered in different counties. The police investigations were handled by different jurisdictions. The only thing the victims had in common was the fact that they were prostitutes who worked regularly at particular truck stops. Each woman had her own trademark, and when she was finished servicing one customer, she would get on his CB radio to solicit her next client, openly advertising her prices and specialties on the air.

The killer apparently intercepted some of these calls, posed as a customer, and arranged for the woman to come to the cab of his rig. One clue has emerged: he may have driven a black or dark blue Peterbilt truck with a sleeper on it, possibly pulling a refrigerated trailer. "Unsolved Mysteries" learned that this serial killer may have used—and perhaps still uses—the CB handle "Dr. No."

"No" is what his victims would have said if he had asked them to leave the truck stop with him. All of these women generally stayed at the stops with their customers. Since they were all found elsewhere later— many of them brutally beaten before they were murdered—it is believed they were killed or knocked unconscious at the truck stop before being dragged away.

REWARD!

Shirley Dean Taylor
Photo courtesy of Ohio Interstate Homicide Task Force

Four of the women are still unidentified. The only identified victim whose family is offering a reward is twenty-three-year-old Shirley Dean Taylor. This five-foot six-inch dark-skinned white woman, weighing 125 pounds, was found spread-eagled, with her panties wrapped around her arm, on July 20, 1986, off Interstate 71 in Medina County, Ohio. She was last seen on July 18, in the rear lot of the Union 76 truck stop in Austintown, wearing a black camisole and pink hot pants.

There's no indication that any of the women knew the killer before their fateful appointment with him, although, one victim, twenty-seven-year-old Ann Marie Patterson, also known as Cindy Lawson or Jenny Morrison, supposedly told the police she had information about the murders but that she was afraid to talk. A few days later, on March 23, 1987, she was found beaten to death in Warren County, Ohio. She had been tossed out in a sleeping bag alongside Highway I-71.

Although most of this killer's earlier victims were found scattered near I-71 in Ohio, later victims also turned up in Illinois, Pennsylvania, and upstate New York. "Unsolved Mysteries" claims that 150 homicides nationwide fit this basic pattern, implying that the same killer may have been responsible for all of them. The program also speculated that the I-71 Killer may once have been a security guard or a police officer, since he is familiar enough with police investigation techniques to know how little sharing of information there is between different counties. That could be why he scattered the women's bodies in separate jurisdictions.

Crimebeat magazine was the first to present the possibility that the Truck Stop Killer could also be the Green River Killer. The theory is discounted by most law enforcement officials, including Sheriff L. John Ribar of the Medina County Sheriff's Department, who was also part of the Ohio Interstate Homicide Task Force on the Truck Stop case. He says the Truck Stop Killer—sometimes called the I-71 Killer—has a distinctly different M.O. "He got rid of his victims without leaving the cab, for they were usually found adjacent to the highway," Ribar points out. "He also did some unusual things with the bodies. For example,

REWARD!

one piece of clothes from one of the victims was found every mile for ten miles."

It was almost as if this killer was saying, "Come and get me." But so far, no one has. He has struck in five, maybe six, states, and perhaps he no longer limits himself to prostitutes. His latest suspected victim was a housewife who went out shopping, disappeared, and has not been seen since. Her car was found off I-71 at a spot where at least two of the other victims were accosted.

The last Midwest murder credited to the killer for certain, another Jane Doe, was in 1990. Interestingly, that's when the killings in Washington started up again, which is why some people there think the Green River Killer has come back home.

REWARD: $28,400
FROM: A fund administered by the King County Major Crimes Office
FOR: Information leading to the arrest and conviction of the Green River Killer
CONTACT: King County Major Crimes Office
                Telephone: (206) 296-7530

REWARD: $10,000
FROM: Ohio Interstate Homicide Task Force
FOR: Information leading to the arrest and conviction of the individual responsible for the murder of the I-71 victims
CONTACT: Telephone: 1-800-282-3784

REWARD: $1,000
FROM: Family of Shirley Dean Taylor
FOR: The arrest and conviction of the suspect in the murder of Shirley Dean Taylor

REWARD!

CONTACT: Medina County Sheriff's Department
218 East Liberty St.
Medina, OH 44256
Telephone: (216) 725-6631
Attention: Detective Wolk or Buralingame

The above information is subject to the warning at the beginning of this book.

REWARD
$5,000

35

I Want My Babies Back!

In November 1987, Susan Zaharias took her children, Christopher and Lisa Mae, from their Mission Viejo, California, home and disappeared. Susan's husband, Louis, the father of the two children, hasn't seen them since. And he has spent every waking moment working to bring his "stolen" babies back.

"I've spent nearly $500,000," Louis says. "I live at the poverty level. I've had two nervous breakdowns, and if it wasn't for my mom and myself pulling together, and the people I work for trying to give me whatever flexibility I can get to pay bills, I wouldn't have been able to survive this."

Each year approximately 350,000 children are abducted by their parents in America. Unfortunately many of these parents take their children not out of love for them but as a means of revenge, to get back at the other parent.

REWARD!

Susan Zaharias
Photo courtesy of Louis Zaharias

Zaharias met his future wife on her first day of work as a law school receptionist. They married—without her parents' blessing—in 1981. Christopher was born in March 1984; Lisa Mae in August 1986. "After Susan had the second baby, she got really bad baby blues," said Zaharias. According to him, she also developed a cocaine and alcohol problem, which eventually caused the family major financial hardship. Her friends later testified in one of the many court cases that she hid her addictions from her husband and that the cocaine she took made her paranoid.

"She was an addict who was spending the children's medical prescription money on coke and not taking care of them," says Zaharias. Young Christopher started missing his speech therapy classes because Susan was using the funds to support her drug habit. By the time the bills began to mount and utility services were canceled, Susan, who was handling the family finances, had wasted away to 85 pounds from anorexia.

She became "angry, hostile, and unresponsive," her husband recalls. "She told people that I was in the Mafia and that I had a contract to have her killed." Zaharias's mother had to move in with the family. And then, on November 20, 1987, Susan and the children disappeared.

Zaharias immediately began calling his wife's family. They had never approved of their daughter's marriage and refused to talk to him. He sued for divorce, and after a long legal battle, he won temporary custody of the children. Permanent custody was granted in 1989, after the divorce was final.

But Zaharias learned that the system wasn't able to return his children to him. Without a homicide, parental kidnapping is treated as a domestic crisis, not something that local, state, and federal agencies get involved in. Zaharias had to hire private investigators, including Tony Pellicano, the celebrity sleuth in Los Angeles, who traced the movements of his children to Michigan, Texas, New Jersey, Wetumka, Oklahoma, and then to Greensburg, Pennsylvania, where Susan's brother-in-law is an Eastern Orthodox priest.

Zaharias is also using the courts, but he recognizes

REWARD!

Christopher Zaharias at age three and a half
Photo courtesy of Louis Zaharias

this could be futile if his children and Susan are out
of the country. "If they are going to go international,
they might be in New Zealand or Australia or England
or Canada. Those are the primary countries where
abductors from the United States go."

Susan's relatives, who are in the oil business, have
"unlimited resources." Meanwhile, the financial toll on
Louis is tremendous. "They try to hammer me into
the ground because they're hoping they can drown me
in paper and I'll fall by the wayside and the case will

go to hell. That's not going to happen as long as I have breath in my body."

Louis says fathers whose children have been stolen become overwhelmed by the system. "I still hear 'It's okay, they're with their mother.' It's not okay! I just keep listening to my children's voices. That is my strength."

Susan Zaharias was born December 5, 1959. She is five feet six inches tall, has brown eyes and a small scar on her upper lip; when last seen, she had strawberry blond hair. Lisa Mae and Christopher are both

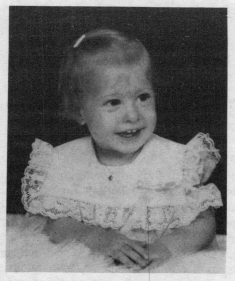

Lisa Mae Zaharias at fifteen months of age
Photo courtesy of Louis Zaharias

blond and blue-eyed. Lisa Mae is now seven; she was only fifteen months old when she was abducted. Christopher is ten; he was three and a half when Susan took him away.

"When I last saw them, my daughter was just beginning to say 'Daddy,' and my son was my best friend."

Louis now lives in Thousand Oaks, California. "Not a day goes by that I don't say, 'Please, God, help us.' I know that this is my test. Sometimes I despair, saying, 'How can you do this to us?' It passes. God knows what he's doing. And I'll just keep praying. Unfortunately, this is an earthly matter, a problem created by people. God had no hand in it."

REWARD: $5,000
FROM: Louis Zaharias
FOR: Information leading to the return of Christopher and Lisa Mae Zaharias
CONTACT: Telephone: 1-800-VANISHED or
(408) 971-4822

The above information is subject to the warning at the beginning of this book.

REWARD
$1,000

36

Happy New Year, Mr. Smith

Don't ever go uninvited to a New Year's Eve party thrown by the sister of Derrick Lloyd—also known as Abdul Aziz—if you want to live, especially if you've had a lot to drink. Don't make threats if you aren't allowed inside. Don't hide your identity when someone comes out looking for you. And don't argue with anyone! Better yet, stay away altogether!

William Smith learned this lesson on January 1, 1991, at about 3:30 A.M. in the Glenwood Housing Project of Brooklyn's Flatlands section. Smith went to the door of Lloyd's sister's apartment. "He demanded to be let in," says Detective Stanley Long of the 63rd Precinct's Detective Squad. Smith "appeared to be drunk and disorderly, and Lloyd's sister would not admit him. After making threats, he left."

REWARD!

Derrick Lloyd a.k.a. Abdul Aziz
Photo courtesy of New York City Crimestoppers Program

Derrick Lloyd, who had become a Muslim and changed his name during one of his many incarcerations, was very unhappy with this reveler. "He went out looking for this New Year's guest," says Detective Long. "He went downstairs and saw this William Smith with a bunch of friends and demanded to know 'where that drunk went.'

"Smith and his friends, realizing who Derrick was, said they didn't know. Abdul got angry and started screaming, 'When I ask a question, I want some answers!'"

Instead of backing down, Smith's friends "told him, 'No, man, you talk like that, you're not going to get

REWARD!

any answers from us.'" At that point, said witnesses, Abdul pulled out a 9mm handgun and fired one shot into William Smith's face.

William Smith is dead; Derrick Lloyd (Abdul Aziz) is at large. "I don't know if he's still in New York," says Detective Long. "Because he's been in several jails and knows many people both within and outside New York State, he may be elsewhere. We've more or less exhausted our avenues of approach locally."

Lloyd was raised in Rockaway Park and may still have friends and contacts there. The local newspaper, *The Wave,* published a Crimestoppers description of Aziz. He is a thirty-two-year-old black male, six feet two inches tall and weighing 200 pounds. He has a light complexion with very pronounced freckles. He frequently wears a black cap, perhaps to mask a receding hairline in the front and on the top of his scalp. He may have grown a beard.

If you run into him, don't let him know that you recognize him. Just call Detective Long right away.

REWARD: $1,000
FROM: New York City Crimestoppers Program
FOR: Information leading to the arrest and indictment of Derrick Lloyd a.k.a. Abdul Aziz
CONTACT: Detective Stanley Long
63rd Detective Squad
Brooklyn, New York
Telephone: (718) 258-4401

The above information is subject to the warning at the beginning of this book.

REWARD
$50,000

37

The Fresno Murders

Dale and Glee Ewell and their daughter, Tiffany, were shot to death in their upper-middle-class ranch-style home in Fresno, California, on Easter Sunday 1992. Their bodies were found two days later by a cleaning woman after the Ewells' son, Dana, became concerned that he couldn't reach his family on the phone.

Fifty-nine-year-old Dale Ewell, a former engineer at Douglas Aircraft, was president and owner of Western Piper Sales, Inc., based at the Fresno Air Terminal. His company sold aircraft for general aviation, and he also owned farms in central California.

Dana Ewell, then twenty and a Santa Clara University finance major, was out of town at the time of the slayings. Suspicion soon fell on him since he was the only member of the immediate family who was not murdered. However, he had the best alibi anybody could ever want: he had been visiting his girlfriend and her parents in San Jose—and her father is an FBI agent.

The murder may have occurred in the following manner. According to the Fresno *Bee*, "Mother and daughter may have been confronted before they walked in the door. Glee was gunned down in the den, Tiffany in the kitchen." Dale was shot from behind as he entered the house, probably unaware that his wife and daughter had already been killed.

An investigation by the Fresno *Bee* turned attention to what appeared to have been unusual, if not questionable, aeronautical business activities on the part of Dale Ewell. The paper speculated about whether the murder could have been connected to his hard-nosed approach to business, pointing out that his company had been involved in twenty-one lawsuits since 1980.

Questions were also raised as to whether he had been involved in equipment tampering—changing the number of flight hours on a plane to mask a marijuana smuggling operation, and whether that could have had something to do with the crimes.

There were also some questions concerning the use of money "raised by Filipinos once tied to the corrupt Ferdinand Marcos regime" for a golf course development that Dale's younger brother had attempted. And the rumor mill went into full gear when it came out that Glee had once worked for the CIA.

Investigators have now begun to answer some of those questions. They've ruled out the drug connection—a speculation tied to Dale's former partner, who

REWARD!

had run a Mexico-to-Fresno smuggling venture back in 1971. Also, while Glee did work for the CIA for a brief time, it was as a Spanish-language translator in Argentina. And it was unlikely that business deals gone sour would have resulted in the murder of Glee and Tiffany as well as Dale.

The police desperately need help on this case. In May 1992 a reward of $25,000 was offered by three relatives of the Ewells for information leading to the conviction of their killer or killers. And in October 1992 that fund was matched by another $25,000, added by the son, Dana Ewell, who is currently running the family businesses.

In Fresno the rumors have quieted from a roar to a subdued whisper. Sheriff's spokeswoman Margaret Mims says, "We're looking at everything and everybody. We can't rule anything or anybody out."

REWARD: $50,000
FROM: Ewell family relatives
FOR: Information leading to the arrest and conviction of the killer or killers of the Ewell family
CONTACT: Detective Ernie Burke or John Souza
Telephone: (209) 488-3932 or (209) 488-3925

The above information is subject to the warning at the beginning of this book.

REWARD
$40,000

38

Driving Through Scottsdale

You may have seen one of the boys who was killed; he was an extra in the movie *Raising Arizona*. If you have the video, he's the one in the football scene wearing sweatshirt number 1, being victoriously hoisted on the shoulders of his teammates. Todd Bogers's burgeoning movie career ended soon afterward because of a minor altercation he and his best buddy, Cory Holmes, had with the driver of another car.

In his home city of Scottsdale, Arizona, twenty-three-year-old Todd Bogers was better known because of his famous stepmother than because of his brief moment in the movies. His stepmother is Patricia Noland, a state senator in Arizona, who was frequently in the news there for her work on behalf of victims' rights. In fact, on December 6, 1991, the night before Todd was murdered, she had again been working late

REWARD!

Todd Bogers and Cory Holmes
Photo courtesy of Patti Noland

on a violent crime case, little realizing that subject would soon hit home.

At 3:30 that morning the phone rang. Half awake, Patricia Noland's husband and Todd's father, John Bogers, heard someone tell him he was to come immediately to a hospital in Scottsdale, more than two hours away. All the caller would tell him was that there had been an accident involving his son, Todd, and Todd's best friend, Cory.

Todd, a business major at the University of Arizona, and twenty-four-year-old Cory had been friends since grade school. They had gone through high school together, played on the same football team, and, at the time of their deaths, worked at the same fitness club. They had been working late shifts to make extra money, and both had been at the club that night until it closed.

Despite the hour of the call, Patricia Noland never expected the worst. "Scottsdale is where you don't expect your child to drive to a party and be murdered," or so Patricia Noland once naively believed. But after their health club closed that night, Todd and Cory had decided to go to the swank Hyatt Regency hotel to catch the end of a party. While they were driving there, they cut off the driver of a white late-model Mazda MX-6 or Toyota Camry with tinted windows, white wheel covers, and black molding along the sides of the body, according to three witnesses who later came forward to say they had noticed some kind of friction between the drivers of the two vehicles at the intersection of Scottsdale and Indian Bend roads. Afterward, the driver of the white car followed Todd and Cory two miles to their next destination. When the boys pulled into the parking lot of the Hyatt Regency Scottsdale at Gainey Ranch, one of the most exclusive areas in Arizona, the killer followed them. It was 1:20 in the morning.

The killer parked so he couldn't be observed and waited until Todd and Cory got out of their car. Then he fired his gun at them three times, hitting Cory in the stomach and Todd twice in the chest. Todd died immediately, slumped next to his car. Cory died on the operating table soon afterward.

Patricia Noland says, "The hardest thing for us has been that the person who did it was so cold and calcu-

REWARD!

**Sketch of suspected killer of Todd Bogers
and Cory Holmes**
Sketch courtesy of Mesa, Arizona, Police Department
and Silent Witness Program

lated. It did not appear that he was high on drugs. The FBI did a profile on him and believe he had professional training with handguns, either as a policeman or in the military. They think this man has killed before and may kill again."

It is assumed that the murderer did not come from Scottsdale, since no one recognized him after the city was papered with fliers. Based on the account of an eyewitness in the parking lot, the killer was dressed in a black sport coat, white shirt, and dark slacks. He was a Caucasian of medium build with a thin waist,

REWARD!

about twenty-five years old, approximately five feet ten inches tall and 175 pounds. He had short dark wavy hair, which he wore slicked back.

According to the TV show "Prime Suspect" five days after the murder a woman called the Scottsdale police saying she was at a private party in Laughlin, Nevada, where she claimed to have overheard a man boasting that he had shot two boys after they cut off his car. The caller said she believed this man's name was Gary.

Gary, if that was the killer's real name, probably didn't hang around Scottsdale for the funeral, missing the dual ceremony in which the two boys, best friends from childhood, were buried side by side.

REWARD: $40,000
FROM: Bogers and Holmes Reward Fund
FOR: Information leading to the arrest and prosecution of the suspect in the murder of Todd Bogers and Cory Holmes
CONTACT: Telephone: Silent Witness (602) 261-8600
or write John Bogers or Patricia Noland
Box 30042
Tucson, AZ 85751

The above information is subject to the warning at the beginning of this book.

REWARD
$100,000

39

The Killer in the Russian Fur Hat

On November 15, 1991, a few days before he was killed, twenty-seven-year-old Richard Germany, a Brink's bank messenger from Detroit, told his childhood friend that he was afraid for his life. Expressing his fears for the future, Germany predicted what he felt was his inevitable death on the job, the Detroit *News* reported later. But there was nothing Germany could do: the holidays were coming up, bills were pouring in, and there were no other job prospects on the horizon. Besides, he valued the friendships he had made at work. "He would always say it was like a family down there on the job," says his sister, Marshell.

His family—both his real family and his office family—lost Richard Germany during a daytime robbery perpetrated by a man wearing a Russian-style fur hat.

REWARD!

According to the police and the FBI, Germany was shot twice at point-blank range at about eleven o'clock in the morning as he was leaving the Security Bank and Trust Company on Telegraph Road near Thirteen-Mile Road in Bingham Farms, Michigan. Germany was taking a canvas bank bag with $38,000 in cash and four bags of coins to the Federal Reserve Bank in Detroit.

His killer never gave him a chance. One fatal bullet pierced his heart and lung. Germany stumbled outside the building toward the armored truck and collapsed, his own gun still clipped in its holder. He died at Providence Hospital in Southfield.

The killer was described by witnesses as a black male, about five feet nine, weighing 150 to 160 pounds.

Composite drawing of Richard Germany's killer
Sketch courtesy of Franklin Village, Michigan, Police Department

REWARD!

Distinctive features were his Russian-style fur hat, long beige trench coat, and dark-framed glasses. After the robbery and shooting, the killer fled the office building through a rear door with the cash. No one saw a getaway car.

The crime is being investigated by Michael Gearty, FBI special agent in charge of the case, and locally by Franklin Village detective William Castro.

Ten days after the crime, Brink's, Inc. offered a $100,000 reward. Martin Crowe at Brink's says, "Richard Germany would have handed the man the bag if the killer had waited a few seconds." Detectives have theorized that the thief may have been known to Germany or perhaps he just wanted to make sure Germany didn't identify him later. "It was a cold-blooded shooting," Crowe says. "Germany never reacted, never had an opportunity to defend himself."

Detective Castro says, "We did receive several leads and calls about look-alikes," with a Russian-style fur hat and non-standard-looking glasses, but they went nowhere.

"We strongly believe there is someone out there who has information," continues Castro, "but for some reason that person is not coming forward. This happened in broad daylight in a highly populated area, a crowded building, close to lunchtime. People were coming in and out.

"Knowing the way these individuals operate, I believe this person, if he acted alone, must have told someone what he did. I don't think he kept it to himself. It's not usual for criminals to keep things to themselves. They brag."

REWARD!

REWARD: $100,000
FROM: Brink's, Incorporated
FOR: Information leading to the arrest and conviction of the murderer of Richard Germany
CONTACT: FBI Special Agent Michael T. Gearty
Telephone: (313) 879-6090 or (313) 965-2323

The above information is subject to the warning at the beginning of this book.

REWARD
$1,000

40

The Palm Sunday Abduction

Most children who disappear permanently are later found to have been murdered shortly after their abduction. What worries most parents is what happened in between. Horrifying questions arise, of the sort that the mother of Richard Chadek III keeps asking herself: "Was he terrified? Was he tortured? What was he forced to do?"

In discussing Richard's case, Detective James Wilson of the Omaha, Nebraska, Police Department, says, "It appears the child was taken care of for a week," small consolation to Theresa Chadek, who finds that her child's death permeates not only her thoughts but her relationships as well.

"The hardest part is when someone asks you if you have kids," Richard's mother says. "It's amazing the reaction that question evokes—embarrassment, hurt. It's a very painful reaction to an innocent question."

REWARD!

She still feels this discomfort even though it's been eight years since she lost her son, years in which the killer of eleven-year-old Richard has remained at large. Her son disappeared at about five o'clock on the afternoon of March 23, 1986, while riding his bicycle home from a friend's house. Theresa Chadek, who was divorced from Richard's father, began to search shortly thereafter. She found his bike in a bank parking lot at the corner of Forty-second and Valley streets in Omaha.

Eight days later a farmer found his body lying in a ditch by the side of the road in northwestern Douglas County, Nebraska. The cause of death was traumatic asphyxia, probably due to strangulation or smothering, according to police reports.

More than six thousand people were interviewed, but the only clue was a blue pickup truck seen in the bank parking lot the afternoon Ricky disappeared. "There are some very unusual circumstances in this case as to the condition of the youngster's body," says Detective Wilson, who does not want to reveal more, except that they were investigating certain individuals outside of Omaha.

Ricky's father, Richard Chadek, Jr., has a new family and is finishing medical school in his hometown. He is a former police officer, as were Ricky's grandfather and uncle. "One of my instructors was at Ricky's autopsy, and he assured me that Ricky wasn't sexually assaulted," he states. The father is comforted at least by that thought.

Richard Chadek, Jr., because of his own experience as a policeman coupled with his family background, is better able to consider his son's fate objectively. He thinks maybe the person who abducted his son "was a little crazy and wanted to have a companion, a young child. And when it didn't work out, for whatever reason, he killed Ricky. Or maybe it would have been a white slaver situation, or perhaps it was getting too hot for the abductor, so rather than risk going forward, he just dumped Ricky."

Lieutenant Tony Mohatt, who investigated the case from the day of the boy's disappearance that Palm Sunday weekend in 1986, knew and worked with the dead boy's family. "We don't ever want to close the case," he says, "until we find the killer."

REWARD: $1,000
FROM: Omaha Crimestoppers
FOR: Information leading to the arrest and indictment of the person responsible for the abduction and murder of Richard Chadek III
CONTACT: Omaha Crimestoppers
           Telephone: (402) 444-STOP

The above information is subject to the warning at the beginning of this book.

REWARDS
$10,000
$20,000

41

Wiped Out in Woodside and Whitestone

Laura Gossmann's worst fears about New York City turned out to be true on the morning of December 22, 1991, when someone strangled her and left her in a deserted gully in the borough of Queens. "People thought maybe she had been too compassionate and had stopped to talk to a dangerous homeless person or a drug addict, because she'd briefly worked in a homeless shelter when she was at school in Nashville," says her mother, Susan, referring to a volunteer job her twenty-three-year-old daughter had in college, feeding and comforting the homeless.

But when Laura returned to New York, "she didn't trust the homeless up here because many of them are alcoholics and druggies and nut cases," her mother contends. That's what makes the only real clue found in this case so confusing.

REWARD!

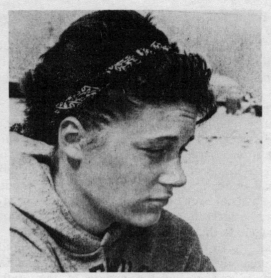

Laura Gossmann
Photo courtesy of Susan Gossmann Casey

Dogged police work by New York City detective Jim Christopher unearthed a photo that may be of Laura, taken by a surveillance camera she probably passed right before she was killed, but the photo—of two figures—is so hazy and grainy, it's hard to be sure.

"It could also be Santa Claus, as far as we know," says the mother. "I wake up one day and wonder if it's Laura, and think it's somebody else another day. They don't even know which is Laura in the picture. They felt it was the shorter of the two figures, but it could also be the taller one."

If the person in the picture is Laura, and the person

with her is homeless or a drug addict, it's highly unlikely she was voluntarily walking along the street with
him. "She had told me on a few occasions, including
the night before she died, that New York scared her
because of the crime that was going on," her mother
says. "Our neighborhood, Woodside, used to be considered safe, but now we have drug problems."

Laura, who had gone out late Sunday morning, was
found strangled a few hours later six blocks from her
home in a deserted factory area on an embankment
between the Brooklyn-Queens Expressway and the
Conrail tracks at Thirty-fourth Avenue in Woodside.

She had not been raped, and the only sign of a strug-
gle was a laceration on her chin. "She would never
have gone to that place on her own," her mother says
firmly. "It can be pretty isolated there, especially that
time on a Sunday morning. I know grown women who
wouldn't go there in the middle of the weekday
afternoon."

Susan has hired a private investigator, Dan Kelly of
Bo Dietl & Associates, to do supplementary work on
the case. Kelly explains that in an investigation like
this, "it's important to reexamine the scene at a time
similar to when the crime occurred.

"This neighborhood is different on a Sunday morning than during the week," he explains. "Certain stores
are closed, people are going to church, weekend jog-
gers may come out, different family members are
walking the dog, and any of these people may have
seen something."

Thus, on Sunday mornings, Dan Kelly re-interviews
the weekend people in Woodside—especially the ad-

dicts who he believes will provide the best clues to the crime. "Particularly if one of them gets off drugs or gets into a compromising situation with the law," he says hopefully.

Another victim lived in Whitestone, Queens, generally considered a safe area—although there may be no such thing anymore. In 1991 there had been a rash of burglaries around the red brick home of Mary Jane Malatesta, but while others near her house at 160-14 Twenty-seventh Avenue locked themselves in, Mary Jane trustingly continued to leave her front door unlocked or even open while she was working.

In December 1991 Mary Jane Malatesta was so excited she must have felt as if nothing could touch her. For two years she had waited to adopt a baby. Finally, she and her husband of ten years, Carmine, were expecting their long-awaited child who was to arrive before the end of the year.

That day, the door of Mary Jane's house was open to let in the light; she probably felt secure because she had locked the screen door, although the bolt was so weak the slightest tug could open it. Maybe that's why there was no sign of forced entry after she was murdered that morning while she was cleaning the basement rec room, which she and Carmine had been preparing for their child.

She was found with two bullet wounds in her head from a small-caliber weapon. Oddly, both rounds went into the same hole, indicating that the gunman had a steady hand and was knowledgeable about weapons. She had been shot from a distance of at least five feet,

REWARD!

Mary Jane Malatesta
Photo courtesy of Carmine Malatesta

for there were no powder burns, and the two bullets had been fired in rapid succession. Some of her jewelry had been taken, but her purse was nearby, untouched. Her husband Carmine's jewelry was gone, and his bureau drawers had been ransacked.

In this kind of a homicide, the spouse is generally the prime suspect. The police were immediately suspicious of Carmine, but he passed a lie detector test. Independent studies have shown, however, that polygraph machines, even in the hands of so-called experts, are only about 50 percent accurate—about the same as tossing a coin. More important than the results is whether the person *wants* to take a test—and Carmine volunteered to do so. He also put up a reward and hired a private investigative firm, Bo Dietl & Associates.

Vincent Pepitone has been working on this case free of charge because he's known Carmine Malatesta for years. His suspicion is that the murder was done by a close male friend of the Malatestas with whom they had a falling-out. That friend was furious at Mary Jane for encouraging his wife to leave him because he was abusing her. Mary Jane's warning that the husband was dangerous appears to have been well founded because that man is now in jail awaiting trial for the murder of a drug dealer. But he wasn't in jail when Mary Jane was murdered.

Of course, there were also all those other burglaries in the neighborhood. In fact, just about anyone who was on that street in Whitestone that day could have killed Mary Jane Malatesta. After all, the door was open. And so is this case. . . .

REWARD: $10,000
FROM: The 34-43 60th Street Owners Corporation and friends and family of Laura Gossmann
FOR: Information leading to the arrest and conviction of the person or persons responsible for the murder of Laura Gossmann
CONTACT: Richard "Bo" Dietl
         Telephone: (718) 424-9366 or (718) 396-4422
         (24 hours)

NOTE: Final determination of eligibility and payment of this reward will be made by the above-mentioned and not by the New York City Police Department.

REWARD!

R E W A R D : $20,000
F R O M : Carmine Malatesta
F O R : Information leading to the arrest and conviction of the person or persons responsible for the murder of Mary Jane Malatesta
C O N T A C T : Richard "Bo" Dietl
              Telephone: (718) 424-9366 or (718) 396-4422
              (24 hours)

NOTE: Final determination of eligibility and payment of this reward will be made by the husband of Mary Jane Malatesta and not by the New York City Police Department.

The above information is subject to the warning at the beginning of this book.

REWARD
$25,000

42

The Vanishing Des Moines Newsboys

It doesn't make sense how a nice community like Des Moines would have two paperboys delivering papers two years apart and both come up missing," says Detective James Rowley of Des Moines, Iowa. Twelve years after Johnny Gosch, Jr., of West Des Moines vanished, and ten years after Eugene Martin of Des Moines seemed to have been spirited away from his paper route, "we know no more today than we did twenty-four hours after they disappeared," Rowley says, shaking his head in discouragement.

John Gosch was twelve years old. At the time of his possible abduction on Sunday morning, September 5, 1982, the five-foot-seven-inch, 140-pound, blue-eyed, brown-haired newsboy was delivering the Des Moines *Sunday Register.*

REWARD!

According to Detective Lyle McKinney of the West Des Moines police, "The first indication to the parents that anything was wrong came when they received a call later in the morning from people who reported that they hadn't received their paper.

"Gosch's father—John, Senior—went to his son's route and found his wagon sitting on the sidewalk with the papers still in it. John, Senior, went back and told his wife that he couldn't find his son, and then he went out and delivered his son's papers." The police were notified shortly thereafter.

John Gosch, Jr.
Photo courtesy of Des Moines *Tribune*

The second boy, thirteen-year-old Eugene Martin, disappeared two years later, on August 12, 1984. "It was almost like a replay of September fifth all over," Johnny Gosch's father said after Eugene's disappearance. "We can feel what the parents are suffering, what the boy is going through. We wish the parents and the boy good luck. We know they need it."

Detective McKinney, the investigator in the Gosch case, spoke to Detective Rowley, who would handle the Martin case. McKinney "told me exactly what was going to happen as if this was a blueprint of his case," Rowley said. "And he came within a day of predicting everything."

Detective Rowley continues, "Eugene was seen talking to a white male described as someone who 'could be his father.' There was nothing suspicious about it." Yet, in a matter of twenty minutes this second newsboy disappeared from the corner a few blocks from where he lived with his father and his stepmother on the south side of Des Moines.

Detective Rowley says, "Eugene got up that morning at four-thirty, left his house at five. Between five-forty-five and six-o-five he was seen folding papers and talking to a man on the corner.

"Between six-ten and six-fifteen the bag was on the ground with ten folded papers in it and Martin was gone. When calls started coming in from people missing their papers, the paper manager went out and found the bag, looked for the boy, delivered the papers, and didn't start looking for [Eugene again] until eight-forty. Then we got called in," says the detective.

Eugene's father, Don Martin, believes the person

REWARD!

Eugene Martin
Photo courtesy of Des Moines *Tribune*

who abducted his son "might have been watching him for some time and saw the opportunity to do something." Usually he wouldn't have had such an opportunity because Gene's older stepbrother delivered the papers with him. "Except that Saturday night, Gene's stepbrother went to a party," and the next morning Gene delivered the papers alone. "And that was the last time we saw him."

Eugene was five feet tall, weighed 105 pounds, and had dark brown hair, brown eyes, and a dark complexion; when last seen, he was wearing blue jeans, a gray midriff shirt with white stripes and red sleeves, and blue tennis shoes with white diagonal stripes.

There are similarities between the two cases. "There's a gut feeling they're the same," says Rowley. "But to prove it, I'd have to have a confession from whoever took them or was involved in the abduction, if there was an abduction."

Rowley was surprised to learn recently that there have been a shocking number of abductions in the once-placid Midwest. "I went to an 'Unsolved Homicide' seminar a couple of months back for law enforcement officers from the Midwest. There are many juveniles and adults missing this way. . . . They just disappear off the face of the earth."

Even though he found that his case was not that unusual, it really frustrates him. "I was able to track a gun all over the United States. But I can't find a missing paperboy. It's very frustrating to me," he says, sitting at his desk with a big poster of the Martin child right next to it, which he "swore would never come down until I find this kid."

REWARD: $25,000
FROM: The Des Moines *Register and Tribune*
FOR: Information leading to the whereabouts of Eugene Martin or Johnny Gosch
CONTACT: Des Moines *Register*
Box 957
Des Moines, IA 50304
Telephone: (515) 284-8000

The above information is subject to the warning at the beginning of this book.

43

The Disappearance of Dail Dinwiddie

Since she disappeared I have walked those two blocks hundreds of times trying to figure out what happened," says Dan Dinwiddie, the distraught father of twenty-three-year-old Dail Dinwiddie. "From the bar to the nearest phone is a walk of only three and a half minutes. She didn't disappear voluntarily," he quickly adds. "She was at a crossroads in her life, but she was happy and looking forward to her future."

But now Dan Dinwiddie and his wife, Jean, wonder whether Dail will ever have a future. On September 24, 1992, their five-foot-tall 96-pound daughter was last seen in Columbia, South Carolina, at around one-thirty in the morning. Dail had gone to join some high school friends at Five Points, near the University of South Carolina campus. They were to meet at a local hangout called Jungle Jim's at 724 Harden Street.

REWARD!

Dail Dinwiddie
Photo courtesy of Dan Dinwiddie

Dail was seen talking with two of her friends there, and then the doorman saw her leave. Her father says, "We don't know whether she found a ride outside with someone she was acquainted with or whether she was going to a public telephone to call me to ask me to pick her up. Jungle Jim's doesn't allow the patrons to use the telephone, so she may have been going down the street to use a pay phone."

Her father, an independent insurance agent, explained that "we have always had a good relationship in our family. Dail knew that if she wanted a ride home, she could call me or her mother at any time of the day or night and we'd come get her. That's why we think she may have gone to the pay phone."

REWARD!

Or perhaps she met someone who offered her a ride home. "She wouldn't have gone off with a stranger," her father insists. "If she did go off with someone she didn't know, it wouldn't have been voluntary. She's feisty and would have fought."

Her father firmly believes that she did not leave Columbia of her own volition, even though she felt uncertain about her future. She had studied art history, a hard field in which to find work even during good times. During a recession it was extremely difficult. Still, she had decided to stick with the field and do what she loved anyway. "She had finally decided to go on and get a master's degree at the University of South Carolina School of Art History," says her father proudly, adding that Dail had been relieved and happy about her decision.

Discouraged, he let his voice trail off. "We don't know any more than we did on September twenty-fourth. We just know many people who were *not* involved" in the disappearance. Their daughter had a dimple, blond-streaked light brown shoulder-length hair, and brown eyes.

REWARD: $50,000
FROM: Dan and Jean Dinwiddie
FOR: The safe return of Dail Dinwiddie
CONTACT: Telephone 1-800-843-5678 or contact
Columbia Police Department
Lincoln St.
Columbia, SC 29201

The above information is subject to the warning at the beginning of this book.

REWARD
$10,000

44

The Coney Island Killer

The seven hundred fifty token booths of the subway system are miniature banks. Every day about four million dollars in small bills go through the token booth windows," says Jared Lebow, a spokesperson for the New York City Transit Authority.

Robberies are an accepted part of the business—there's an average of one a day—but the three murders of token-booth clerks in two years have alarmed the city. And police have few clues to the latest, the murder of Russell Manzo, at a Coney Island stop in January 1993.

Things like this weren't supposed to happen. "A few years ago people who were desperate for money started to break into turnstiles," says Transit Workers Union Local 100 Vice President James A. Mihalics.

The turnstiles "were reinforced, and we fought to get improvements. Now a booth has become something of a fortress."

Still, that didn't help Russell Manzo. He worked at the Van Siclen stop, which is deserted at night. The F train that stops there serves many apartment complexes, including the Trump Houses, built and managed by entrepreneur Donald Trump's father.

At this stop, sometime between 12:50 and 2:00 A.M. on January 5, 1993, Russell Manzo was shot to death during a robbery. His body was discovered at 2:30 A.M. by a police officer on routine patrol. The policeman noticed that the door to Manzo's mezzanine-level booth was closed but unlocked, which was unusual. When he looked in, he saw Manzo's body curled up on the floor.

It was immediately obvious that a robbery had taken place. The forty-one-year-old clerk had been shot in the chest and throat inside the $250,000 fiberglass-and-steel stronghold built to withstand robbery and all kinds of assault. Police say the weapon was a semiautomatic, but they don't know why the door was unlocked. "There was no reason for anybody to go into that booth at that time of the morning," says New York City Transit Police Detective James Nuciforo. "There was no relief expected, and no meal relief. We know from speaking with people in the area and people who knew Manzo that he was very cautious in the booth. That just adds to the mystery as to how that door was opened."

What Transit Police were able to learn was that someone—perhaps with a key—got access and may have followed Manzo back into the booth after a token collection.

"It's very hard to tell because there were no witnesses," Detective Nuciforo adds. "There were some homeless people in the station, but they were sleeping at the time. The murderer may have been somebody Manzo knew, so we're digging into his background. We're interviewing everyone he knew or had dealings with."

So far, nothing in Russell Manzo's background would indicate that anyone would want to kill him. He was a dedicated man who took care of his legally blind wife during the day. He began working as a token clerk in February 1987 and was assigned to various locations, most of them in Brooklyn. He was transferred to the Van Siclen station four months before his death.

"All you have going through that station at night are the security guards from the nearby buildings who work from four P.M. to midnight," says Detective Nuciforo. "You have a handful of people coming off the train at two A.M. Activity doesn't increase until four-thirty or five A.M., when early-shift workers head for Manhattan."

The Transit Authority is currently planning to phase out the tempting token-booth fortresses and substitute electronic card devices for entrance into subways. Whether this will reduce overall crime in the subways is debatable. Where there's money, someone will always find a way to take it.

REWARD: $10,000
FROM: Transit Workers Union, $5,000; New York City Transit Authority, $5,000

REWARD!

FOR: Information leading to the arrest of the killer of Russell Manzo

CONTACT: Transit Workers Union
Telephone: (212) 873-6000
or Detective James Nuciforo of the New York
City Transit Police
Telephone: (718) 834-7201

The above information is subject to the warning at the beginning of this book.

REWARD
$10,000

45

Lights
for Laurie

Laurie Depies vanished from a parking lot in Menasha, Wisconsin, on August 19, 1992, a disappearance that has been compared with the fictional abduction in *The Silence of the Lambs*.

With a colleague from work, the twenty-year-old, who liked Stephen King novels and was interested in Eastern religion and fashion, had walked to her gray 1984 Volkswagen Rabbit at a shopping mall in Grand Chute, Wisconsin. Most probably, she then drove to her boyfriend's apartment in Menasha, about six miles away.

He heard her car's noisy muffler at about 10:20 P.M. as she pulled into the parking lot. The car was found parked less than forty feet from his second-floor apartment. When Laurie failed to come upstairs, her boyfriend went down to look for her. He found only her

REWARD!

Laurie J. Depies
Photo courtesy of Town of Menasha, Wisconsin,
Police Department

locked car, a plastic soft drink cup on its roof. Laurie was never seen again.

Town of Menasha Police Chief Weiss stresses that "No one saw her get out of the car. They heard her car drive into the parking lot, but they never saw *her*. We don't have any idea what may have happened," he says. "Really three different scenarios are what we're basing our investigation on. One, she was forcibly abducted by a stranger. Two, she left of her own volition with somebody she knew or thought she knew. Three, she just decided to leave."

REWARD!

Weiss says, "She is basically an average twenty-year-old midwestern young lady. She doesn't have anything detrimental in her background that would lead us to believe that she herself may be involved in any improper activity. The people who she associates with are average twenty-year-old midwestern people."

At the time of her disappearance she was wearing a black sleeveless turtleneck shirt, black and white shorts, and black shoes. She is five feet five inches tall and has brown hair and green eyes.

"I have my days where it's like the day after," says Laurie's father, Mark, who lives in Fond du Lac. "I feel helpless, hopeless, angry because of nothing happening. It gets worse every day," he says resignedly. "I can't mourn, since I have nothing to mourn for. We have no information. I feel she is still alive and being held. I'm just totally emotionally drained."

One small comfort for him and Laurie's friends was provided by the Fox Valley communities and reported by the Milwaukee *Journal-Sentinel* and *Post-Crescent*. "It is a family tradition to light a candle on Christmas Eve to light the way for the Christ child," said Jean Lorenz of the Aid Association for Lutherans. "I thought perhaps if members of the community could light one candle in their windows the evening before Christmas Eve, the Depies family might feel a community hug and know that we're thinking of them even in the midst of our holiday preparations."

And so in a country where a staggering number of victims are frequently ignored and forgotten, the people of this community put candles in their windows to give one of their own a symbolic hug. Her friends and

REWARD!

neighbors didn't want Laurie Depies to become just another statistic; even if she turns out to be one of the 25,000 or so murder victims in the United States each year, at least the people in her community showed that they cared.

REWARD: $10,000
FROM: Family of Laurie Depies
FOR: Information leading to the identity of those responsible for the disappearance of Laurie Depies
CONTACT: Town of Menasha, Wisconsin, Police Department
Telephone: (414) 739-2333
Laurie Depies Volunteer Search Center
Telephone: (414) 729-0490

The above information is subject to the warning at the beginning of this book.

REWARD
$100,000 (Canadian dollars)

46

Someone Is Killing the Babies!

There were those who believed a maniac was on the loose; others charged that nurses were being used as sacrificial lambs. But two things are certain about the death of forty-three babies in Toronto's world-renowned Hospital for Sick Children: it was an incredible calamity, and one or more people—yet unidentified—murdered many of those infants with lethal doses of digoxin.

The first suspicious case occurred in the cardiac ward at Canada's foremost children's health facility on June 30, 1980, where eighteen-day-old Laura Woodcock died; the last death occurred less than a year later, on March 22, 1981, when three-month-old Justin Cook passed away. The deaths were all linked by the fact that they occurred in the same cardiac ward under similar nursing teams and that all of the autopsy reports concluded that in each baby digoxin levels were high enough to kill an adult.

"Digoxin was supposed to be there," according to Tony Warr, a Metropolitan Toronto Police sergeant assigned to the case along with Staff Sergeant Jack Press. Digoxin is a form of digitalis, and regulates the strength of the heartbeat, but the levels were inexplicable. "All of these patients were on the cardiac ward, and digoxin is a common cardiac drug—as common as aspirin but for cardiac ailments," he explains. "There are few patients for whom it is contraindicated, for whom it would do more harm than good. But an overdose of it will kill anybody."

By March 1981, nine months after the first deaths were reported, the coroner brought hospital officials and the homicide squad together, and they started looking at nursing schedules and logs. Suspicion immediately led to the arrest of nurse Susan Nelles. She seemed an unlikely suspect, since her father was a respected Ontario pediatrician, her brother was a doctor at the same hospital where she worked, and she was an experienced nurse, but Nelles was charged with giving massive doses of digoxin to some of the babies, resulting in their death.

Sergeant Warr points out the "startling" fact that "from the day we made the arrest, there was not a death for six months on the ward, and then [the death rate] went back to its normal expected amount. These are very sick patients, so some were expected to die."

After a forty-four-day preliminary hearing in 1982, Susan Nelles was set free. Says Sergeant Warr, "The judge at the end of that preliminary hearing decided that there wouldn't be enough evidence to convict her."

Judge Vanek said, "All of her actions are perfectly consistent with the due and proper performance of her regular duties as a registered nurse."

When the revelations of the deaths began to hit the press and television, the Canadian public was hardly prepared for the communications blitz. "It was just amazing," says Warr. "The media attention was unbelievable. It was front-page news for a long, long time."

In fact, a year later there was *another* inquiry, headed by Justice Samuel Grange. The Grange Commission hearings were spread over sixteen months in 1983 and 1984 with sixty-four witnesses. The hearings were carried live on cable television, and many Canadians were all but glued to their TV sets.

One of the highlights of this second inquiry was the appearance of Susan Nelles herself in May 1984. During her testimony, virtually *no* one left his or her TV set. Her defense focused on the possibility that a crazed murderer had been loose in the cardiac ward. Nelles also admitted she had a "strained relationship" with another nurse, and someone might have wished to discredit her.

Judge Grange dismissed any suggestion that the overdoses were accidental or the result of medication error. For him, it was "against all common sense" to accept the idea that the same accidents or errors could have taken place repeatedly with the same nursing teams on the same ward. Nevertheless, Nelles was again exonerated.

Each year a reward of up to $100,000 Canadian dollars is renewed for this case. Constable David Boothby of the Metropolitan Toronto Police says, "If somebody came forward with information that was acceptable in court that resulted in a conviction, my recommendation would be that the whole hundred thousand dollars be paid."

The only person so far to receive any money is Susan Nelles. In 1985 she was awarded $190,000 in damages for malicious prosecution and negligence. Today she is married to a city official and the mother of three.

REWARD: $100,000 (Canadian dollars)
FROM: Metropolitan Toronto Police
FOR: Information leading to the arrest and conviction of the person or persons who murdered the babies at Toronto's Hospital for Sick Children
CONTACT: Tony Warr, Metropolitan Toronto Police
Telephone: (416) 324-6150

The above information is subject to the warning at the beginning of this book.

REWARD
$10,000

47

The Death of a Policeman's Daughter

At one time even the most violent crimes didn't disturb police officer Jim Marable. "I just did my job and never was really that affected by what I saw. I looked at it like 'try to find out who did it, and then get the hell out.'"

But all that changed for the twenty-year veteran of the Nashville police force because of what happened on September 9, 1990, to his nineteen-year-old daughter, Jamie. That day she was found dead of multiple stab wounds in the neck and chest, her body so badly decomposed that medical personnel couldn't even tell if she had been raped.

Officer Marable received a call from another police officer four days after Jamie disappeared. "He asked me if my daughter was still missing. Then the voice said, 'We've found a girl in Fort Royal, Tennessee.' My

REWARD!

Jamie Marable
Photo courtesy of Regina E. Austin

heart stopped. 'She is badly decomposed,' he said. 'We think it's your daughter.'"

Marable immediately read all the police reports on Jamie, "but there was one report I said would never read," he says today. "I finally read it, and it said she didn't have any eyes left when she was found."

The last time Marable and Jamie's mother, Mrs. Regina Austin, had seen her, Jamie was going to a party for her sister at the Golden Jukebox on U.S. 79, in Clarksville, one of her favorite hangouts. Jamie was in a restless mood when she arrived, however, and after an hour she left to see what was happening at a club nearby.

Jamie returned to the Golden Jukebox around 2:00 A.M., to find that her sister had left. She then learned that while she was at the other club, a cousin had come along and a fight had broken out. Someone had hit her cousin over the head with a beer bottle, and the young woman had been rushed to a hospital for treatment, accompanied by Jamie's sister.

Alarmed, Jamie told people that she needed a ride to the hospital. At 2:30 she was seen for the last time ever in the parking lot of the Golden Jukebox, talking with a man about five feet eleven inches tall, 275 pounds, muscular, with darkish skin, driving a dark blue GMC Silverado truck. The truck was seen leaving the parking lot at the time she left the Golden Jukebox.

While doctors were putting sixty stitches in her cousin's head, Jamie's sister nervously waited at the hospital. When Jamie still hadn't shown up by 7:00 A.M., her sister knew something was wrong.

The police sergeant who investigated the disappearance told the Nashville *Banner,* "The investigation was difficult from the get-go because of the girl's friends." He explained that several key witnesses to the events that night were uncooperative or told stories that did not match.

At the time of her disappearance, Jamie was wearing jewelry that was not found on her body: a yellow-gold band ring, size 6 or 7, with a black onyx stone and a diamond slash across the center, and a black watch with a semi-oval face and yellow-gold trim, a small diamond set at 12, dashes at 3, 6, and 9, battery operated, with a yellow-gold watch band, ¼ inch wide. Knowing the whereabouts of this jewelry could be helpful in finding the killer.

Meanwhile, Marable believes he will not be able to get over Jamie's death until an arrest is made. "If it was a car wreck I could go on with my life," he says sadly. "But this way I can't. My doctor told me, 'Forget about Jamie.' I said, 'Doctor, you tell me how to do that and I will, but I can't.' People don't understand."

In the meantime, Officer Marable feels that his experience has changed his attitude toward other crimes. In fact, he now works full-time with Crime Stoppers in Nashville. "Just the other day we got a murder case," he says. "A girl was abducted, and I keep thinking about her. What happened to me has made me more aware of how the families are feeling. I feel more for their grief—and know how long it stays with them."

Something that has stayed with Jamie's mother for a long time is a conversation she had with her daughter two weeks before she died. "Jamie had a premonition that death was imminent," said Regina Austin. "A few days before she died she said that if anything ever happened to her we should play 'Stairway to Heaven' at her funeral," Mrs. Austin recalls. "This has bothered me ever since. Was it a coincidence or was she trying to tell me something? I'll never know for sure."

One thing is certain: There was scarcely a dry eye when "Stairway to Heaven" was played at Jamie's funeral.

REWARD!

R E W A R D : $10,000
F R O M : Family of Jamie Marable
F O R : Information leading to the arrest and indictment of the person or persons who murdered Jamie Marable. All calls are confidential.
C O N T A C T : Telephone: (615) 645-TIPS

The above information is subject to the warning at the beginning of this book.

48

The Yogurt Shop Murders

What especially bothered the mother of two of the teenage girls who were murdered in Austin, Texas, on December 6, 1991, was that the killer also set fire to the yogurt shop in which the bodies were found, so her two daughters were burned beyond recognition. "We never got to see them again," says Barbara Suraci, referring to her two daughters, Jennifer Harbison, age seventeen, who worked in the shop, and her fifteen-year-old sister Sarah, who had dropped by. Also killed with Jennifer and Sarah were Eliza Thomas, seventeen, who was also employed by the yogurt shop, and Amy Ayers, thirteen, who was visiting.

The conflagration started right before midnight at the I Can't Believe It's Yogurt shop at 2949 West Anderson Lane in the Hillside Center in north Austin. There had been trouble at this small twelve-store

Jennifer Ann Harbison
Photo courtesy of Barbara Suraci

Sarah Louise Harbison
Photo courtesy of Barbara Suraci

Amy Leigh Ayers
Photo courtesy of Pam Ayers

Eliza Thomas
Photo courtesy of Maria Thomas

shopping mall before. One shop on that strip had been broken into eight times in the previous two months, forcing the owners to put bars in the windows.

But I Can't Believe It's Yogurt took no such precautions, even though the store was highly vulnerable, because they utilized unsupervised teenage help, and stayed open until 11 to accommodate patrons of the nearby movie theater who might want a snack after the final showing.

The firemen who responded to reports of the blaze and entered the store didn't see the bodies of the four teenagers. Only when they got to the back of the shop did they find the remains of the Harbison girls and their two friends.

All four girls had been shot in the head, probably in a robbery. It appeared that the killer or killers then set fire to the store in an unsuccessful attempt to mask the murders. "Murder is pretty senseless anyway, but this one was even more so because it was multiplied by four," says Sergeant Investigator John Jones of the Austin Police Department.

"We did a risk assessment on the victims, looking for possible 'risk factors' precipitating the crime. The only risk factor present was the closure of the business at night," says Jones.

Not only don't the police know for sure why the girls were killed, they also don't know exactly how many murderers there were. "There is no description of the killers because there are no known witnesses," he says.

Those who were out for blood on this case—and that included most of Austin—were mollified somewhat a year later when two men who had formerly lived in Austin were arrested for an unrelated crime in Mexico and a warrant was issued for a third suspect. Mexican officials—followed by the media—proclaimed that these men were also guilty of the "yogurt shop" murders.

One of those arrested, Portofiro Villa Saavedra, nicknamed "the Terminator," is the leader of a sixty-member motorcycle gang known as Mierdas Punks. According to Mexican officials, Saavedra has ties to international drug trafficking rings and other forms of organized crime. Arrested at the same time was twenty-two-year-old Alberto Jiminez Cortez. The police are still looking for twenty-six-year-old Ricardo Hernandez, nicknamed "the Witch" because of his hooked nose.

But Jones stresses that it has not been established that these men were responsible for the yogurt shop crimes. "A lot of people are under the assumption that two guys in Mexico did it and we're just waiting to find the third one. That's because the Mexican government said the two men confessed, and they did, but I'm not sure what they confessed to," says Sergeant Jones, adding that "the reported confessions are still under investigation."

Interestingly, within two days of their "confession," both men recanted, and during their arraignment, one man said that he had been tortured by Mexican federal agents. While all evidence points to their guilt in a kidnap and rape case in Austin about two weeks before the yogurt shop murders, there's no evidence of their involvement in this crime.

REWARD!

"They're bad guys and we thank law enforcement that they caught them," says Frank Suraci, a forty-one-year-old manager for a computer company and stepfather of the Harbison girls. "But we can't get close enough to these men to find out if they're the ones responsible for our case," he says. "The leads on our case have dwindled from five thousand to five hundred. It's been a real roller coaster for us," he says frustratedly.

REWARD: $125,000
FROM: FRIENDS OF SAJE Inc.
FOR: Arrest and conviction of the person or persons responsible for the murder of Jennifer and Sarah Harbison, Eliza Thomas, and Amy Ayers
CONTACT: Austin Police Department Homicide Division
Telephone: (512) 480-5113

The above information is subject to the warning at the beginning of this book.

49

The Van with the Skier on the Side

A highly unusual van was seen at the time of Cherrie Ann Mahan's disappearance. Anyone who remembers it and knows who drove it might at last be able to help solve this crime. And earn almost $50,000.

So far the disappearance of eight-year-old Cherrie Mahan about a hundred yards from her home remains unsolved. As in many cases like this, waiting—and not knowing—has almost destroyed the family.

Janice McKinney, Cherrie's thirty-three-year-old mother who now lives in Mars, Pennsylvania, says, "At first I just couldn't handle it. I was hurting so bad I started drinking because I just didn't want to hurt anymore." An assistant supervisor of housekeeping at a nursing home in Pennsylvania, she had to take time off as a result of her anguish over the disappearance of her daughter. "I couldn't go home because everything

REWARD!

Cherrie Ann Mahan
Photo courtesy of Janice McKinney

reminded me of Cherrie. I had to stay at other people's houses."

On February 22, 1985, when Cherrie disappeared, her mother was living in Cabot, Pennsylvania. The school bus always dropped Cherry right off in front of the house on Cornplanter Road. From there it was only a short walk up the driveway to the home where her mother would be waiting.

"We lived on top of the hill, and we never saw what happened that day," says Janice McKinney. "We heard the bus come, and we heard the bus stop, and Cherrie should have gotten off, which she did. But somehow she never made it to our driveway."

What made it especially painful for Janice to return to her home after the disappearance was that "we had just bought that place to raise Cherrie so she could ride her bike there and have a good life."

But Cherrie never saw the house again. At exactly 4:05, she turned and waved good-bye to three school-mates who had gotten off the bus with her. They waved back, and she circled around the bus so she could get to her driveway.

Composite sketches of the van and the painting of the skier
Sketches provided by Pennsylvania State Police

REWARD!

One mother was parked in front of the bus, waiting to pick up her child. She happened to look up and see Cherrie in the rearview mirror. She noticed that the four-foot-two-inch, 68-pound girl with a fair complexion, unusually large hazel eyes, and brown hair worn below her shoulders, took a second to straighten her clothing as she got off the bus.

She adjusted her brown Cabbage Patch earmuffs decorated with long hair, rearranged her blue book bag, which had two straps with a cream-colored top and a blue and red heart. When Cherrie walked out of view, she was wearing a gray coat over a blue denim skirt, blue leg warmers, and ankle-high beige boots that her mother had helped her put on that morning.

At that moment the watching mother got a brief glimpse of a dark green or blue van. On the side of the van was a painting of a large snow-capped mountain. In the middle of the picture was the figure of a skier in a red and yellow ski outfit racing down the mountain. The mother noticed that the driver of the van was also wearing ski clothes.

Cabot is a small town, and all of the residents made an effort to find Cherrie. While they failed, the fact that she still hasn't been found keeps Janice McKinney going. "We have hope that Cherrie's alive because often they find these kids who disappear two to three weeks later, dead. And we haven't found anything in all these years. So somebody took her for a reason. We just don't know what that reason was."

REWARD: $50,000
FROM: Friends and neighbors of Cherrie Ann Mahan, Inc.

REWARD!

FOR: The safe return of Cherrie Ann Mahan or the arrest and conviction of the person or persons who abducted her

CONTACT: Pennsylvania State Police
Butler, Pennsylvania
Telephone: (412) 284-8100

The above information is subject to the warning at the beginning of this book.

REWARD
$5,000

50

She Danced with Dave Winfield

Statistically blacks are frequently the victims of crime. What made Bertha Rodgers's death especially sad was that this beloved art teacher was murdered during Black History Month. Forty-seven-year-old Bertha, nicknamed "Be," lived alone in a three-story brick house at 655 West 183rd Street, New York City, only a few hundred yards from the local police precinct.

On February 20, 1987, when Be did not appear at school for the second day in a row, principal Richard Darwick sent an aide and a security guard from her school, Intermediate School 187 in the Washington Heights section of Manhattan, to her home. Darwick had expected Bertha in school that day because she and her students were preparing their display for the Art Connection, a Black History Month exhibition.

REWARD!

They found the door of her house unlocked; Bertha's body was discovered on the second floor. Her hands had been tied with a telephone cord, which was also wrapped around her neck. She had been struck on the head with a ball peen hammer, and a bloodstained hammer lay nearby. There were marks on Be's neck from the telephone cord, indicating that "she may have choked to death," according to the police. Detectives also said some jewelry appeared to have been taken. Principal Darwick says the police investigation was thorough, but the intruder's fingerprints were too incomplete to establish a connection to possible suspects in the neighborhood.

Be was a woman who dressed in bright, colorful turbans and loved baseball. She especially adored Dave Winfield and would take her students to Yankee games just so she could see her idol in action. She used to joke and tell people she'd like to marry Dave Winfield. While she never accomplished that, perhaps the high point of her life occurred when she got to dance with Winfield at a Dave Winfield Foundation party.

Six years after the senseless killing, Ann Eskayo, Bertha's teaching colleague, is still upset. "Every time I think about it, I cry," she says, crying so hard she could barely continue the interview. "All the kids loved her. They were horrified."

Teacher's union president Sandra Feldman said, "Our first reaction was shock, our second reaction was anger, and our third reaction was—we have to do something to help find out who did this." A $5,000 reward was posted by the United Federation of Teach-

REWARD!

ers for information leading to the arrest and conviction of the murderer.

REWARD: $5,000
FROM: The United Federation of Teachers
FOR: The arrest and conviction of the murderer of Bertha Rodgers
CONTACT: New York City Police Department
Homicide Office
Telephone: (212) 598-0071

The above information is subject to the warning at the beginning of this book.

REWARD
$16,000

51

Kristen's Last Day

It began as a wonderful weekend for eight-year-old Kristen Gray. On Saturday morning her mother, Susanne Shirk, had gone to a garage sale and bought her a pair of white shoe-type roller skates with blue wheels. Kristen loved them so much, said the Miami *Herald,* that she didn't want to take them off when she went later that morning to Matheson Hammock Park beach, south of Miami, Florida, with her stepfather, Ron Shirk, and her four-year-old half brother, Stephen.

When they returned from the beach to her stepfather's apartment behind the big Dadeland Mall south of Miami, she spent the afternoon skating—actually, stumbling—up and down the second- and third-floor hallways of the building.

Between 3:00 and 4:00 P.M., Ron was in the communal laundry room, checking regularly on Kristen's progress on her new shoe skates—but the last time he

248

went out to see if Kristen was okay, she was no longer there. Ron immediately started a frantic search. Within hours police officers, neighbors, security guards, and helicopters joined the hunt.

Kristen Gray was next seen sixteen hours later, on Sunday morning, February 4, 1990, when a fisherman discovered her body floating in a rural South Dade County canal, more than eleven miles from Dadeland and three-quarters of a mile north of Homestead Air Force Base. Kristen's body was still clothed in her red sleeveless sundress with white trim. She was barefoot, her beloved roller skates no longer on her feet.

"This is still an open case, regrettably. There are not many we'd like to solve as much," admits Detective Doug Stevens of Miami Homicide. "There are no runs, no hits, no leads."

The happy little blond, blue-eyed, churchgoing Girl Scout had been struck and then choked. She died as a result of "blunt trauma" and manual asphyxiation. There were also "indications she had been hurt."

Detective Joseph McMann of Metro Dade Police was called into the case when the body was found. He reported that "It was difficult to learn anything because of the nature of the injuries and the time of death. There were no witnesses. There was no car, there were no unusual people around. It was a Saturday, so it wasn't possible for people who were there to set time frames exactly.

"We canvassed every apartment complex in the neighborhood where she disappeared," McMann said. "We checked sex crime suspects, perverts. We reached dead ends all along the way.

REWARD!

"And then we widened the search. Once you expand on the immediate area, you've got to be lucky. We weren't," Detective McMann added. "There were no leads. The forensics examination of DNA led nowhere. We never had one legitimate lead, nothing that wasn't a supposition."

No one knows how the killer got from the hallway in the apartment complex to where Kristen was found in the canal on SW 107th Avenue just north of SW 268th Street, a distance of eleven and a half miles. He either took the Florida Turnpike, the fastest and most direct route, or drove down U.S. Highway 1.

Miami and Dade County police and detectives want to put this case to rest. Police offer $16,000 in rewards, including $1,000 from the Crime Stoppers program. The murder of Kristen Gray "has outraged the public," according to a police spokesperson.

REWARD: $16,000
FROM: Metro Dade Police and Miami Crime Stoppers
FOR: Information leading to the arrest and conviction of the killer of Kristen Gray
CONTACT: Crime Stoppers
        Telephone: (305) 471-8477
        or Detective Doug Stevens
        Metro Dade Police
        Telephone: (305) 471-2400

The above information is subject to the warning at the beginning of this book.

REWARD
$50,000 (Canadian dollars)

52

A Prostitute's Final Customer

There's nothing unusual about a cocaine addict turning to prostitution to support her habit, going off with some unknown customer to a deserted area, and later being found brutally murdered. It happens all the time in the United States.

But this happened in Ontario, Canada. And there the police have posted a $50,000 reward, reflecting the greater amount of money and manpower they expend in solving every Canadian homicide, no matter what the victim's station in life.

Regardless of the commitment of the police, this case may be difficult to close. Not much is known about the twenty-year-old victim, Cheryl Nelson, who lived in one of Toronto's rougher neighborhoods. "Formally, her address was with her parents, although she spent a substantial amount of time on the street,"

REWARD!

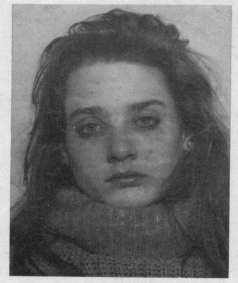

Cheryl Nelson
Photo courtesy of Toronto Metropolitan Police Department

says Detective Paul Allen, formerly with the Metropolitan Toronto Police Department.

"Her drug abuse was an ongoing battle, and unfortunately she could never rid herself of it. It led her to engage in . . . prostitution, and she ultimately paid for her lifestyle," he says.

It was two years before her death that Cheryl first got into drugs. Until then, according to the Toronto *Star,* she had been a good student at her Catholic high school. But around the time of her eighteenth birthday, she went off the right track and on to the fast track, discovering cocaine.

In order to pay for her habit, she turned to prostitution, earning ten to fifteen dollars for each sexual encounter, not enough to allow her to go with her clients to hotels. Most often she had to work out of places like the one where she was found: a factory area in the back of the industrial mall on Eddystone Avenue in North York, Ontario.

Prostitutes frequently went there late at night behind the buildings when the factories were closed. Cheryl was found there on March 9, 1991, savagely beaten and stabbed numerous times, with drug paraphernalia strewn around.

Although no one expects to die like that, Cheryl *was* aware of the dangers of her lifestyle. She had tried more than once to get off drugs, especially since she knew her habit was breaking her family's heart.

A year before she was murdered she had checked into several drug rehabilitation programs. For brief periods she freed herself of cocaine and was again the outgoing, happy young woman she had once been. But she was never strong enough to "just say no" to offers of free cocaine from her supposed friends. Each time, within a month, she said yes, returning to her drug habit and her dangerous way of supporting it.

Unfortunately she had to have contact with a large number of men in order to pay for all the coke she needed. Thus, the police have had a lot of work trying to establish which customers were hers, and especially which was the last one.

"She plied her trade on the street with a lot of people, and her turnover was fairly rapid, although there's no evidence to suggest anything organized along those lines," such as a pimp who might have had something to do with her death, says Detective Allen. "It just seems to have been a trick gone bad."

Allen has reason to be optimistic, however. The police in Canada solve more cases than do investigators in other countries, because the people there care more about doing so. As Cal Millar, police reporter with the Toronto *Star,* says, "In Canada, because we don't have that many homicides, they're not just statistics. People who die have a human face, and the public gets involved rather than just being morbidly curious. They wonder how they can help solve these cases and give the police tremendous assistance."

REWARD: $50,000 (Canadian dollars)
FROM: Metropolitan Toronto Police
FOR: The arrest and conviction of the person or persons responsible for the murder of Cheryl Nelson
CONTACT: Metropolitan Toronto Police
          Telephone: (416) 324-6150

The above information is subject to the warning at the beginning of this book.

REWARD
Unspecified
amount

53

Fire at the Quarry

When firemen responded to what seemed to be a routine fire in Kansas City, Missouri, on November 29, 1988, they never realized they might be walking into a trap. The first report they received had sounded innocuous enough; they were told that a car was on fire on Interstate 87 South and Highway 71.

When the firemen arrived to extinguish the fire in the car, however, they saw there was a second fire in a pickup truck belonging to one of the security guards stationed at a nearby quarry. Since the burning truck was on the other side of the interstate highway, the first group of firefighters called for another pumper company to handle the second blaze.

Security guards at the quarry warned the second group of firefighters to be careful in handling the truck fire across the highway as there could be deposits of dynamite and blasting caps there.

This information was duly noted, but once the second group of firefighters reached the burning pickup truck, they saw a *third* fire, this one in a tractor trailer truck filled with equipment used to blast rocks in the quarrying operation.

Three unexplained fires that had started up so rapidly were cause for concern, as were the bunkers several hundred yards away that contained explosives. But the second company became so engrossed in putting out their fire that they apparently let their guard down.

After the first company had extinguished the initial minor car fire, they joined forces with the second company working on the burning tractor trailer truck, and at that moment an explosion occurred. Not just an ordinary blast, but 25,000 pounds of ammonium nitrate and fuel oil. Six firefighters were killed instantly and several others were injured.

More fire trucks arrived, just in time for *another* explosion as an additional 25,000 pounds of explosive materials rocked the center of Kansas City five or six miles away. People for miles around trembled, thinking that the end had come.

The occurrence of two fires, followed quickly by a third, points to arson. Fire Chief Charles Fisher, director of the Kansas City Fire Department, says the investigation "was pretty active for a while," and he reports that the case is "still open."

REWARD!

R E W A R D : Unspecified amount
F R O M : International Association of Fire Fighters Local
F O R : Information leading to the arrest and conviction of the
arsonists in the Kansas City quarry explosions
C O N T A C T : International Association of Fire Fighters Local
Kansas City, Missouri
Telephone: (816) 921-9407

The above information is subject to the warning at the beginning of this book.

——————————— **54**

Three Young Girls

We have many missing children cases, but they get settled quickly, usually when a kid shows up at a friend's or neighbor's home," says Detective Terry Price of the Pinole, California, Police Department. But Amber Jean Swartz-Garcia, Ilene Misheloff, and Michaela Joy Garecht are just three of several California girls whose cases have not been solved rapidly. The cities of northern California's East Bay—the area east of San Francisco—are waiting for answers.

Amber Jean Swartz-Garcia

It would have been normal for Amber Jean Swartz-Garcia to have stayed very close to home. "It was abnormal for her to have wandered off at all," adds Detective Price. "So there was immediate concern.

REWARD!

Amber Jean Swartz-Garcia at age eight

Amber as she may have looked at age ten
Courtesy of Amber Foundation

She was in the front yard when they [her mother] last saw her. The word 'abduction' is a misnomer. What we have is an 'unwitnessed disappearance,'" she stresses. "We don't know if she voluntarily left. Of course, how does an eight-year-old decide to leave home?" But somehow she did.

At about four o'clock on June 3, 1988, Amber was in the front yard of her Savage Avenue home, jumping rope. Her father, Floyd "Bernie" Swartz, a Pinole police officer, had been killed in the line of duty a few months before she was born. "That made it hard for a lot of officers around here to deal with her disappearance," says Price.

Tim Bindner, whom we discussed in Chapter 6 in connection with the 1991 Nikki Campbell case, played a role in Amber's case as well. Amber's mother, Kim Swartz-Garcia, identified Bindner as a man "who came to the house and offered his help." He also volunteered to help in the search for Amber.

Now, here comes the especially frightening part. One of the notes discovered later in Bindner's van said, "I love you, Amber. You are my first. And I tried so hard for you. I tried and cried and still ache in my heart."

The first what? The first one he searched for? The first one he loved from afar? Or the first—something else?

Amber was four feet tall and weighed 62 pounds. Her eyes were blue, her hair medium blond. Amber suffered from migraine headaches. Her condition wasn't serious, but whenever she had an attack she lost her balance and vomited. She also had a hearing impairment, but she was able to communicate without her hearing aid. She was not wearing the hearing aid when she disappeared.

Ilene Misheloff

Thirteen-year-old Ilene Misheloff generally left school in Dublin, California, at 2:30 in the afternoon. She was excused from regular physical education classes because she was enrolled in an after-school

REWARD!

Ilene Misheloff
Photo courtesy of Dublin Police Services, Dublin, California

ice-skating program. Since her fellow students had one more class than she did, Ilene generally walked home alone.

On Monday, January 30, 1989, she was supposed to be picked up at home by her skating coach for the trip to the rink. She followed her usual route from school, which included walking along a ditch—a dry creek bed near Mape Park. It was a popular shortcut for students headed into the Silvergate residential area where Ilene lived. She was last seen at about 3:00 P.M. on Amador Valley Boulevard near the Shamrock Plaza Shopping Center.

REWARD!

Ilene's parents, her brother, and her fraternal twin are devastated. They still think she will be found, even though standard methods plus search helicopters with infrared devices, a milk-container campaign, local and national media coverage, televised enactments, hypnosis of people who may have seen vehicles along Ilene's route home, and a reward fund of $95,000 have as yet failed to locate her.

A few clues did turn up. According to the local newspaper, the Tri-Valley *Herald,* at the time of Ilene's disappearance one witness saw a van stopped in the fast lane on San Ramon Road north of Amador Valley Boulevard. Several young people were seen outside the van. Another caller described a mid-1980s, light-colored four-door American sedan seen near Mape Park on the day of the abduction.

Ilene was wearing a charcoal gray pullover polo sweater, a horizontally striped pink and gray skirt, and black Keds. She was carrying a dark blue backpack. At the time of her disappearance, she was five feet three inches tall and weighed 115 pounds. Her hair and eyes are brown, and she was wearing braces on her teeth.

Michaela Joy Garecht

Incredibly, nine-year-old Michaela Joy Garecht was abducted right in front of witnesses at 10:15 on the morning of November 19, 1988. The little girl with a blond ponytail was taken from the parking lot of the Rainbow Market in Hayward, California, by a pock-marked white male adult who drove off with her in a run-down car.

REWARD!

That sunny weekend morning, Michaela Joy Garecht and her best friend rode their bikes to a local grocery store on Mission Boulevard to buy candy and soda. They left their bikes in front of the store, and when they emerged, they found that one of the bikes had been moved into the parking lot.

When Michaela went to retrieve it, a man suddenly grabbed her, threw her into a rusty older car, and drove off with her. Several people saw the kidnapper before, during, and after the abduction, but it all happened so quickly that no one got a clear image of him.

The first person to see him was the owner of a 7-Eleven not far from the grocery store. The suspect had bought a cup of coffee there. "I will never forget him," the store owner said after she realized what the man had done.

Other witnesses included Michaela's young friend; a Union City grandmother who was in line behind the two girls and noticed the kidnapper before she entered the store; and the grocery store clerk. A woman who drove behind the getaway car got a glimpse of him, too.

Their combined recollections were that he was a man in his late teens or early twenties, of average height and build with shoulder-length dirty-blond hair and a clean-shaven but pimpled or pockmarked face.

Dennis Oliver, a reporter for the Alameda Newspaper Group, which owns the Tri-Valley *Herald,* says the police believe that fate worked in his favor. For example, the videotape for the 7-Eleven's surveillance camera was being rewound at the exact time the abductor was buying coffee, so there was no photo of

REWARD!

Michaela Joy Garecht
Photo courtesy of Hayward, California,
Police Department

him. And there were no fingerprints in the 7-Eleven because the place was cleaned right after the abduction, before anyone realized the suspect had bought coffee there prior to the kidnapping.

Then, a garbled emergency call transmitted the wrong information about the kidnapper to the police. The abductor was described as in his thirties with a mustache and as driving a burgundy-colored car. And the woman who was driving behind the kidnapper kept quiet for four months before she came forward, perhaps because the wrong description of his car had

REWARD!

**Composite sketch of suspect in
abduction of Michaela Joy Garecht**
Courtesy of Hayward, California,
Police Department

been widely publicized. By the time she spoke to detectives, her memory had already faded. Hayward Police Detective Ken Gross figured that the kidnapper needed fifteen seconds and "all the luck was on his side and none of it on ours."

"We don't know what's going on here," says reporter Oliver. "All we know is that kids disappear every now and then and are never seen again. I've tried to figure out a scenario," he says. From the abductor's appearance "and the appearance of the car, and the way the act was perpetrated in broad daylight—in front of witnesses—you must have someone who's on drugs or who's emotionally disturbed. He got away with it because he's lucky. He's probably a pedophile. I would imagine the girl was probably killed within the first day. And he probably hid the body real well."

Michaela was wearing a white T-shirt with the word "Metro" across the front and pictures of people near the midsection. Her denim pants were rolled above her knees. She wore three-inch pearl or white-colored earrings that resembled dangling feathers.

The composite drawing of the killer is very similar to the composites created with the help of witnesses for many other abductions around the United States, says Michaela's father, Rod Garecht. He sees his daughter's kidnapper as being responsible for perhaps a dozen other kidnappings coast-to-coast. He mentions the abduction of a child in Oceanside, California, as one of many by an identically described young man. He surmises that the abductor could be a kidnapper-for-hire, recruiting young girls for prostitution in a well-organized and protected association.

Reporter Oliver disagrees. "With conspiracies where the child is still alive and someone is still holding her, it doesn't seem to me that anyone with any level of sophistication would have hired this man to take the child in his beat-up old car and looking like that. I believe she's dead, lying out in the hills waiting for someone to find her."

Rod Garecht's thinking is admittedly influenced by the revelations of John W. DeCamp in his 1992 book, *The Franklin Cover-Up: Child Abuse, Satanism and*

REWARD!

Murder in Nebraska. DeCamp, a Nebraska State Senator for sixteen years, hypothesizes a nationwide child prostitution ring in which politicians, bank presidents, police officials, newspaper publishers and other powerful people are covering up pedophilia, satanic sacrifices, pornography, and international prostitution in sinister ways.

What can children do to be safer? Chip Haught, coordinator of a Teenage Assault Awareness Program in Ilene Misheloff's town of Dublin, says they "should listen to that funny little voice inside that says, 'This doesn't feel right.'" And Ilene's father, Mike, reminds children not to go into places where people can't see them, like the ditch Ilene may have used as a shortcut.

Other tips from Dublin's Assault Awareness program suggest that children walk home from school with others and let parents know their route home; that they not give out home addresses on the phone or tell anyone that no one else is home; that they not wear any clothing that shows their name. They recommend that children scream loudly if someone tries to touch them and that they run away and tell their parents immediately; that they never accept rides from strangers, even if they claim to be friends of the family, unless they use a code word known only by the child and the parents.

Perhaps some believe children can't get away from an abductor if he is determined to get them, but the truth is that "about a hundred thousand kids get away from stranger/abductors each year," according to John Walsh of "America's Most Wanted" on "Geraldo." "Those are the smart kids, the lucky kids." He added that "there are about forty-six thousand *successful* abductions, but most of those kids are returned. They may be physically or sexually abused or molested, but most of them are gotten back alive.

"But each year," added Walsh, "there are about three hundred unsolved nobody-knows-what-happened-to-them long-term missing kids. Some say three hundred kids a year isn't much. I say if there's three hundred police or three hundred journalists or three hundred anchormen missing a year, it would be a big problem. And I say this: If it was your kid, one of those three hundred, it would be a big problem."

REWARD: Unspecified
FROM: The Amber Foundation
FOR: The return of Amber Jean Swartz-Garcia
CONTACT: Child Quest International, Inc.
        Telephone: 1-800-248-8020
        Hot Line: (510) 724-9066
        or The Amber Foundation
        Telephone: (510) 222-9050

REWARD: Up to $95,000
FROM: The family of Ilene Misheloff, the Alameda Newspaper Group, and many other sources
FOR: Information leading to the recovery of Ilene Misheloff
CONTACT: Dublin, California, Police Services
        Telephone: (510) 833-6670 or 1-800-635-6306

REWARD: Up to $188,000
FROM: The state of California, the Alameda County Deputy Sheriff's Association, the family of Michaela Joy Garecht, and an anonymous donor
FOR: The arrest and conviction of the offender and the return of Michaela Joy Garecht dead or alive

REWARD!

C O N T A C T : Hayward Police Department
Telephone: 1-800-222-3999
or San Francisco FBI
Telephone: 415-553-7400

The above information is subject to the warning at the beginning
of this book.

It's no wonder John Saul called Ann Rule "the undisputed master crime writer of the eighties and nineties." This #1 <u>New York Times</u> bestselling author has become <u>the</u> authority when it comes to writing about society's most twisted minds.

ANN RULE

IF YOU REALLY LOVED ME
76920-0/$5.99

A ROSE FOR HER GRAVE
and Other True Crime Cases
Volume 1
79353-5/$5.99

EVERYTHING SHE EVER WANTED
69071-X/$5.99

Available from Pocket Books

POCKET BOOKS

Simon & Schuster Mail Order
200 Old Tappan Rd., Old Tappan, N.J. 07675
Please send me the books I have checked above. I am enclosing $_____ (please add $0.75 to cover the postage and handling for each order. Please add appropriate sales tax). Send check or money order–no cash or C.O.D.'s please. Allow up to six weeks for delivery. For purchase over $10.00 you may use VISA: card number, expiration date and customer signature must be included.

Name _____

Address _____

City _____ State/Zip _____

VISA Card # _____ Exp.Date _____

Signature _____ 999